RIGHT OF PASSAGE

SURVIVING SHAME AND
BATTLING BULLIES OF ALL AGES

MARY A. RAUCHENSTEIN

AUTHOR ACADEMY elite

RIGHT OF PASSAGE

MARY A. RAUCHENSTEIN

RIGHT OF PASSAGE

SURVIVING SHAME AND BATTLING BULLIES OF ALL AGES

Copyright © 2018 Mary A. Rauchenstein

All rights reserved.

Printed in the United States of America

Published by Author Academy Elite
P.O. Box 43, Powell, OH 43035
www.AuthorAcademyElite.com

All rights reserved. No part of this publication may be reproduced, stored in a retrieval system, or transmitted in any form or by any means—for example, electronic, photocopy, recording—without the prior written permission of the publisher. The only exception is brief quotations in printed reviews.

Paperback ISBN-978-1-64085-082-8
eBook ISBN-978-1-64085-083-5
Hardcover ISBN-978-1-64085-084-2

Library of Congress Control Number: 2017910831

DEDICATION

This book is dedicated to my husband, Paul, who taught me years ago that being nice is free—it doesn't cost you a dime. I also dedicate this book to the families of those who've lost loved ones because of bullying. Together, our voices remain strong, and I have faith that we will be heard.

Contents

Foreword xi
Introduction xiii

Part I: Target Practice

Chapter 1   "At Seventeen" ("I learned the truth at
            seventeen..."). 3
Chapter 2   "Sunday Morning Comin' Down". 12
Chapter 3   "In My Room". 17
Chapter 4   "Wooly Bully" 24

Part II: Victim to Victor

Chapter 5   "Mean Girls". 31
Chapter 6   "You've Got a Friend" 38

Chapter 7   "Voices"............................. 46
Chapter 8   "Help!".............................. 52

Part III: Join the Revolution

Chapter 9   "Crazy"............................. 59
Chapter 10   "Twist and Shout".................... 68
Chapter 11   "Doctor, Doctor".................... 74
Chapter 12   "Take This Job and Shove It!".......... 79

Appendix

A. Action Plan....................................89
B. Bullying Myth Busters 91
C. Definitions of Bullying........................93
D. Resources 95
E. Join the Revolution............................97
(Write your congressperson.)

Acknowledgments 99
In Memoriam......................................101
Endnotes 103

Foreword

If I were to survey any number of random strangers, I guess that most would admit to being bullied as a child. At minimum, most would admit to having witnessed acts of bullying. Sadly, it still seems to be viewed by many as a rite of passage. The unfortunate reality is that for many people, bullying doesn't cease after childhood.

Bullies may have left the playground, but they are present in all facets of our society. Worse yet, as we learned with the massacre on April 20, 1999, at Columbine High School near Littleton, Colorado, some bullies are actually "bully-victims." Those who have been bullied become the bully.

When Mary first sent her book proposal to me, I realized that other books might be more eloquent. However, I also realized that this book has the potential to save lives. I told her it *needed* to be written.

As Mary points out in this book, bullying needs to stop. However, if it doesn't, it could lead to serious psychological damage and potentially death by suicide. The dirty little secret that victims of bullying share is shame. And shame is one of the most destructive human emotions.

I encourage you to read this book if you are a parent and then read it again with your child. Whether you are raising awareness, comforting a victim, or reaching a potential bully, the result should be the same. Bullying needs to stop, and victims need to speak up!

Whether you are a child, a teen, or a middle-aged worker, everyone is entitled to the *right of passage*!

Kary Oberbrunner—Author of *ELIXIR Project, Day Job to Dream Job, The Deeper Path,* and *Your Secret Name*

Introduction

Too many of us have encountered the playground bully. Too often, those taunts are ignored as a simple childhood rite of passage. The problem is that the bullies have left the playground and have infiltrated every corner of society. They are leading companies, churches, and—some might even say—our country.

At one point, I left a company with no anxiety or second thoughts. It was time to go. I got a call one day from one of my former coworkers. He wanted to meet for coffee. He wanted to understand why I left. Didn't I like my job? I liked my job all right; I just didn't like my bully-boss.

I've rewritten this introduction so many times that I bet I could wallpaper any room in my house with those drafts. After reading an earlier iteration, my husband said that it seemed unfocused. He was right! Then he read my first chapter, and I was sure that I'd redeemed myself. Wrong.

He lovingly explained to me that I sounded like a bitter, angry woman who's been holding a grudge for decades. Then it hit me. He was right. I was still holding a grudge from years ago, even though I'd convinced myself otherwise.

Like some of you reading this book, I was bullied from an early age. My bullies throughout school reminded me how imperfect I was. In fact, I let them define me. In retrospect, they were as imperfect as I was, but I did not realize that until many years later. I allowed their voices to get inside my head.

Our subconscious mind is incredibly powerful, and as a professional coach, I believe that our subconscious mind is the key to unlocking unbelievable and almost unimaginable human potential. But to actualize our potential, we may first need to do some cleanup. You see, one of the things I've learned is that bullying leaves deep wounds and scars. Until we address those, moving forward will be difficult, if not impossible.

It's like trying to put a fresh coat of paint on a badly rusted piece of steel. Steel is one of the strongest metals, yet if not properly scraped and brushed, a fresh coat of paint won't cover up the rust spots that lie beneath the surface. In time, if the spots are not intentionally treated, they will again be exposed.

I realized that my soul was like steel. Sure, I could be tough on the surface and be seemingly unfazed by life's events, but deep down in my subconscious mind, I'd never brushed or scraped the wounds left from childhood, which were rusting my soul. I still believed the bullies' lies that I was a worthless speck of dirt. I was holding on to a truckload of rotting residue.

Even though it's always been difficult for me to accept any type of compliment, I believe that some of the positive words of encouragement offered to me over the years were like sandpaper gently scraping off that rust. They didn't completely eradicate the scars, but they helped me to understand and to begin to believe that I *was* someone who mattered, just as you are. You see, as human beings, we innately possess a sense of value and purpose, but I had allowed my childhood bullies to strip that away. But hey, those days are over, so no more bullies, right?

Introduction

You can imagine my surprise when my naïveté and optimism were challenged upon graduating from college. Only then did I realize that bullies may have left the playground, but some were now occupying key leadership roles in companies. It took some time, but I came to the realization that enough was enough, and I learned to stand up to a few of them.

Like some of you, I experienced bullying in a variety of environments, including school, church, a doctor's office, and at work. As tough as it has been for me personally, I've learned that forgiveness and laughter—accompanied by acceptance and celebration of our own uniqueness—is the best way out. I believe it's the *only way* to maintain your self-esteem and happiness.

But that's only part of the recipe; we also need to remove bullies from positions of leadership until they learn to adjust their behavior. And I'm not convinced that punishment alone is an effective long-term solution. It certainly plays into vindication of sorts, but punitive measures won't necessarily be long lasting when it comes to helping adults to make behavioral changes.

Victims of bullying often struggle with the effects of these long-lasting wounds. Some experts have compared these emotional scars with those of posttraumatic stress disorder. My desire in writing this book is first to create a greater awareness of the detrimental impact of bullying. Those who are in positions of leadership should be highly motivated to ensure that bullying ceases. Second, I desire to wake up those bystanders who witness bullying. It's time to step up and advocate on behalf of the victims.

I believe that we are all put on this earth to help others—whether one is a parent, a teacher, a relative, or a friend. Pay attention to your loved ones and your students. Look for signs of emotional changes in others. Don't wait until it's too late.

And parents, you are empowered to stick your nose in your children's lives. If your child is suddenly in social overdrive when he or she generally has been highly introverted, what's causing that? If your child is generally very social and suddenly retreats to his or her bedroom for refuge, interrupt that child and ask some questions. Schedule time with your children, and *spend* quality time with them.

While my introduction to bullying began at a very early age, I guess I was lucky not to endure the same level of bullying that many kids go through today. Cyberspace has taken bullying to a new level, and while it is clearly worse now, I can't minimize what I went through. You see, I was bullied every day in high school. Yes, *every day*. So, while we didn't have Facebook, Twitter, blogs, or even e-mail back then, I knew what it was like to be personally humiliated daily. Bullying may have been on a different scale, but it was still bullying; and it was degrading, demoralizing, and demeaning.

Regardless of where bullying takes place, you should never condone or sit idly by as bullies torment their targeted victims. This is vitally important, especially if you are in the human-resource profession or a leader in a company—and by leader, I mean someone who is responsible for influencing the right outcomes, getting results, and holding others accountable. But never do it in an intimidating or threatening manner.

Human-resource professionals and leaders need to realize that bullies are often broken people themselves. We are probably all broken people, when you think about it. But bullies have some deeply rooted, disturbing need to make themselves look good or feel better by controlling their victims and by making them look bad or feel bad about themselves. In a word, it's *control*. Okay, maybe they are two words—*power* and *control*.

If you are a survivor of bullying, celebrate your recovery and help others. You know all too well what it feels like to be alienated and lonely. To those bullies who are perhaps reading this book—*stop* the bullying! Get help. The gig is up. You have a deeply rooted reason for bullying, and your life will continue to be less than fulfilling until you come to grips with your own emptiness.

I tire of those who wish to sweep *bullying* under the carpet or pretend that it's just a normal part of life. A rite of passage. Part of growing up. Critics state that the term is overused and

Introduction

misused, and to that I say, "Really?" Not only does bullying exist, but our society also seems to show signs of becoming immune to it. Too many people are passive observers, allowing it to unfold right before their eyes. And as I state in chapter 11, I most likely would not be alive to write this book if I hadn't stood up to someone who was trying to bully me in a very indirect manner.

I've recently read criticism of those who've come before me in trying to raise awareness about bullying. Some think we're softhearted, thin-skinned crybabies. Hmm…well, please read on, my friends. Imagine if these pages were written by *your child, your sister, your wife, your brother, or your mother?* Mistreatment and intentional intimidation of others should never be acceptable. To those who have been bullied, my hope is that you will use laughter and love to heal the internal scars that have never vanished. And then be strengthened never to let yourself fall victim again.

This book is organized into three parts. Part I: "Target Practice" is where bullying starts for many of us—as kids. It should come as no surprise that an estimated 40–80 percent of school-age children are bullied. Why do some end up being the targets of bullies while others remain untouched? Why do we condone childhood bullying as a rite of passage for those who bully? Regardless, it's important to put yourself in the shoes of those being bullied and help to stop it. To do anything less is inhumane, because the psychological toll that bullying takes on an individual is devastating.

Part II: "From Victim to Victor" details my journey in recognizing that bullies who were once on the playground are now running companies or holding leadership positions throughout society. One can either wrestle internally with the long-term negative impact of bullying or rise above it and defeat the negative voice in one's head that replays the hurtful, negative messaging from the past. It may take years (as it did for me) to undo this damage, but it's necessary for one to live a happy and fulfilling life. And it's worth it—*you're* worth it.

Part III is aptly titled "Join the Revolution." No weapons are needed; just courage, compassion, and a commitment to letting bullies know that enough is enough. It's not okay to stand by idly while a coworker is bullied by another—or even bullied by his or her boss. It's not okay to allow anyone to attempt to control or coerce you through demeaning and humiliating conversation, tone, or body language.

Bullying in the workplace, like sexual harassment, should be illegal. I believe that it will be someday. Until then, policies need to be written, and we all need to be held accountable to them. The bottom line is that effective leaders do not resort to bullying. There are constructive ways to influence others without resorting to destructive means.

Nelson Mandela said, "Education is the most powerful weapon you can use to change the world." To that end, I've included some questions for reflection at the end of each chapter. These questions are ideal if the book is being used for a mastermind group (facilitated peer learning), youth group ministry, or in leadership training in business.

Lastly, I'm a vocalist. No, not a particularly talented one, or I'm sure you would have seen me on *The Voice* by now (as I'm a little too old for the last season of *American Idol*). But music was my salvation as a kid. When the days became unbearable, my sister and I would listen to Elton John, Bobby Sherman, The Beatles, and The Partridge Family (actually, we were only interested in David Cassidy, *not* the entire Partridge Family), and more. Music was soothing to my soul. So, I went back to my roots and incorporated a few catchy song titles as chapter headings to foreshadow the pages that detail my story. And who knows, maybe your purpose will be to write your own story one day so that others have hope. Regardless, are you ready to join me in the revolution and claim your own *right of passage?*

PART I
Target Practice

1

"At Seventeen" ("I learned the truth at seventeen...")

The Playground Bully

Envision a beautiful summer day. The sun is shining; the sky is blue, and a gentle breeze makes a bicycle ride so inviting. Then envision two young girls having stones hurled at them as they ride their bikes on an elementary-school playground. You can almost hear the bully's taunts: "I hope you fall off and break your leg! Do you know how ugly you are?"

The first bully I remember is someone whose name will be forever imprinted in my memory. There's no point in disclosing it, as I believe *that* would be a form of bullying, since the incident occurred more than fifty years ago, and this guy may not even remember what he did to my sister and me. And hey, he may also be dead, and it's not fair to pick on dead people (unless, of course, you're able to fully communicate with them, but that's a completely different book, which I didn't write). Hank (not his real name) lived right next to the elementary school that my siblings and I attended. I had five older brothers and one younger sister. My brothers were truly protective of my sister and me, and for that, I was most thankful.

When my sister and I would ride our bikes up the hill to our elementary school, this kid would taunt and tease us from his yard. He would call us names and make fun of us. Our last name (Bush) was always an easy target for teasing. Well, one of my brothers had heard about the taunting that was being directed at us far too frequently. So, one afternoon, he followed us to the school playground.

There were multiple levels at this school on which you could ride your bike and multiple ways to stay out of view, if you wanted that. Our brother chose to stand on the middle level of the school grounds; he was completely out of sight to our nemesis. Sure enough, Hank started calling us names, throwing small stones at us, making fun of our last name, and generally antagonizing us from the safety of his backyard—which was adjacent to the best place on the school grounds to ride bikes.

I wish I had been able to capture on film the look on Hank's face when my brother emerged and told him that if he ever taunted us again, he would answer to him (my brother). Hank ran like lightning into his house. Just a few moments later, his dad came out and started yelling at my brother. He told my brother to stop picking on his son. My brother told the man that his son had better stop picking on his sisters. He told the father that he had watched and listened to unprovoked taunting, name-calling, and stone throwing directed at us by his son. He told the father to keep his son away from us. Hank's father retreated and went back into his house.

I can only imagine what must have transpired in that household after that discussion. Odd as it may be to believe, that kid never bothered us again on that playground. My sister and I were elated, and we learned a valuable lesson that day:

stand up to bullies. (Of course, it does help to have someone with you who is bigger and stronger than your bully is—like an older brother!)

My Gym Teacher

I've always been an intuitive person. Even at an early age, I knew that one of my elementary-school gym teachers didn't like me. Here's the backstory.

I think that it was President Kennedy who, back in the 1960s, first implemented directives for physical-fitness testing in schools. I'm sure this gym teacher was trying to earn the gold medal in this category, as he took this directive quite seriously.

When I was a child, I had asthma and allergies and was overweight. My family doctor assured me that I would thin out in just a few years and grow out of my asthma and allergies. Guess what? I didn't thin out (until I took control of my diet), and I still suffer from activity-induced asthma and seasonal allergies. Running outside was as impossible for me then as it is now. Imagine having your lungs reduced to the size of a pinhole and trying to breathe normally after you've been running around vigorously. Or, as in those TV commercials for chronic obstructive pulmonary disease (COPD) medication, imagine trying to breathe with an elephant sitting on your chest.

My dad would generally write a note asking the teacher to excuse me from running during gym class when it was "running season." Every time I handed my gym teacher the note, he would announce it to the entire class. "Oh, what a surprise. Mary has another excuse for gym class today. Do you have a stash of these that you keep at your desk?"

One day, it was raining, so I didn't need the note. I kept it in my pocket and thought, "Good; I'm off the hook. No embarrassment for me today." This may sound strange, but although I couldn't run outside or do pull-ups, I could do sit-ups and push-ups like the best of them. I remember acing some of those physical-fitness tests we had to take and feeling good about it.

Hard as it may be to believe, on rainy days, we got to exercise in the school cafeteria—the very room that we'd be eating in just a few hours later. *Yum.* Can you just imagine the fragrant combination of perspiration and meat loaf?

Well, on this particular rainy day, my gym teacher stood on the small stage in the cafeteria and directed us to do any number of calisthenics. Instead of running, our gym session was filled with jumping jacks, sit-ups, push-ups, and more. I loved those days because I could generally keep up with the other kids. I didn't feel like an outcast!

I can only assume that our teacher was trying to instill teamwork in us, as he would not let us move to the next group of exercises until everyone had completed the same set. For example, if you completed all of the sit-ups, we were required to lie on the mat until everyone else had finished. The teacher would always let us know when it was time to move on. For push-ups, we were required to hold our bodies in a plank-like position until everyone had completed the set.

At one point, during this class, more than a few minutes had passed since most had completed the required push-ups. After a few minutes, everyone's arms were ready to break. Yet we had not been released from the plank position. That meant someone had not yet completed the set. Yep, the teacher explained that we could later thank the *one* person who had not yet completed ten push-ups. I have no clear memory of hearing anything, but suddenly, our teacher told everyone to lie down on the mat and rest for a minute.

He then proceeded to hand out paper to everyone in the gym class and told them all to write a letter of apology to me—*me!* I was stunned. More embarrassment. Evidently, someone in the class thought that I was the one who was dogging the push-ups and holding everyone back. But it was not *me.* While my gym teacher didn't reveal who it was (amazingly enough), he once again drew the attention of the entire class upon me.

Before the class was over, he collected the letters of apology and handed them to me. I remember reading a couple of the notes. It seemed that even though I hadn't caused the delay, my classmates still thought it was my fault that they had to write those letters.

While I can't say that my gym teacher really inspired me to a life of healthy living, I will never forget that teacher's name and the message that being different (i.e., having allergies and asthma) was something to be embarrassed about. That teacher eventually transferred to another school, and I hoped that he wouldn't deflate the spirits of too many other kids. Little did I know that he would come to look like an absolute prince compared with what was coming in just a few years.

At Seventeen

I've read that many bullies have also been bullied in life. That must have been the case for a classmate who tormented me in high school. I believe he was in my homeroom all four years of high school, because we were organized alphabetically by last name. Every day for four years, he made sure that he told me how fat and ugly I was.

As a woman in her fifties, I can tell you that while I may want to relive certain years of my life, there is *no* year in high school I'd ever like to repeat. I didn't really have a mom to teach me how to dress, take care of my hair, or wear makeup. As one of my nieces would say, I was undoubtedly "a hot mess."

I was heavy in my freshman year, but I lost eighty pounds during my sophomore year. At almost five feet nine, I weighed less than 120 pounds. I still felt "fat," though, because my self-image was still being dictated by those voices from the past. I realize now that I was relatively fit at that time. I was in the marching band and exercised every day in the basement of my house to keep the weight off. I was too embarrassed to exercise outside for fear that I'd be called fat and ugly again. That's why the lyrics of Janice Ian's song "At Seventeen," really resonated with me:

*I learned the truth at seventeen
that love was meant for beauty queens...*

While my weekdays during the school year started with a constant replay of "fat and ugly," occasionally a popular girl who usually sat next to us would tell our classmate to stop being so mean. That effort turned out to be useless, but I was secretly so appreciative that she at least noticed what was going on and tried to stop it. I often wondered why our homeroom teacher didn't walk around the classroom. It seemed that once attendance was taken and we stood for the Pledge of Allegiance, it was simply a waiting game until the bell rang to move to our first-period classes.

I was tempted to fight back in my junior and senior years by telling him that he was a pathetic, pot-smoking jerk. I'm glad I didn't try to fight fire with fire because I doubt it would have had an impact. I grew to feel sorry for this guy, and eventually I began to talk back to him without insulting him personally. I'm sure my words didn't faze him, but I felt better by speaking up. I felt emancipated by merely sticking up for myself.

The Bully Who Was Disabled

As if the antics I endured in homeroom weren't enough, during my sophomore year, a guy who was legally blind decided to steal my purse during a class. Seriously, I couldn't make this stuff up—a blind kid stealing my purse. In reflection, there really was humor in that. I know that other kids picked on this guy all the time, and I'm guessing that he'd had enough and decided to find his own target. I'm speculating that his logic was "bully or be bullied." He and I were in a history class together. Our teacher was an affable kind of guy, but he had no awareness of what was going on in the classroom. He was in a zone, and it wasn't *our* zone.

My sight-impaired classmate and I were seated in the last two desks in a row next to the windows. I'll never know if other

"At Seventeen" ("I learned the truth at seventeen…")

classmates saw him do it, but I knew that he had to have been the culprit. I had my purse when I went into class; after class, it was gone. No one else could have reached it.

Tired of being a target, I took matters into my own hands. My father was the president of the town council, and I knew a few things about the local police. I'd heard my father recounting stories from time to time. Fortunately, this occurred back in the day when there were actual phone books and landlines. While some phone numbers were unlisted, most of us had numbers that *were* listed. Lucky for me, this kid's phone number was one of those.

I called his house, disguising my voice, and asked to speak to him. He came to the phone and uttered, "Hello."

I made up a false name and told him that I was a detective with the police department. I told him that I had received three phone calls from his classmates who saw him steal Mary's purse.

He fell for it. He panicked, denied it, and then stated that he didn't mean to do it.

I told him that he had exactly two hours to return the purse to Mary with everything intact, or he would be going to jail.

This kid and his mother arrived at our house at about six o'clock. My father had no knowledge of this, and I hoped to keep it that way. Unfortunately, my father came home early (for him) that night and was there when my classmate and his mom arrived. This kid's mom was a good person. I believe she was the den mother for a local Cub Scout pack. She dragged her son into our house and made him apologize, and he returned what he could of the contents of my purse. I didn't have anything of value in my purse other than my house keys, and he did return those. His mother made him buy me a new wallet and gave me a few bucks to buy a new purse.

My dad stood in silence as this unfolded. When they left, I told him what had happened and how I had trapped the boy into confessing to stealing my purse. My dad was very tough on all of us, but he managed to let me know how proud he was of me for doing that. I thought perhaps I might have a future as either a detective or an actress, but I decided not to press my luck. I had other ideas in mind for my career.

First Impressions Are Lasting

Studies show that 40–80 percent of school-age children have been exposed to bullying.[1] They've either been bullied or witnessed bullying. Research also shows that bullying can have long-term effects, some of which have been likened to post-traumatic stress disorder.[2]

I recently completed a journey with my friend and fellow author, Kary Oberbrunner, where it became apparent to me that the bullying I endured did indeed have a lasting impact on me. I was holding on to many names that I allowed to be stamped on my soul for more than forty years. These names included *fat, ugly, loser, friendless, unworthy,* and *victim*.

I've also learned through my professional coaching certification process (which included several hours of online coursework) that our subconscious mind accepts input and holds on to beliefs like a dog holding on to its favorite bone (with luck, not a human's leg). Years of programming (i.e., beliefs that you are fat, ugly, etc.) can't just be undone because people suddenly tell you you're beautiful. That's why it's important to raise awareness about bullying and its lasting impact.

Bullies are people too, and they need help. I'm not advocating that we gather them up and send them to a deserted island to live out the rest of their days. I'm saying that as a society, we must speak up and address bullying when it occurs.

I'll take it one step further. I'm also advocating that we pass legislation (starting at the state level) that is comparable to those laws that make sexual harassment an actionable offense. Bullying, like sexual harassment, should be illegal in the workplace too. While several states have introduced bills that would outlaw bullying at work, as of the writing of this book, no state has *passed* such legislation and made it a law.

"At Seventeen" ("I learned the truth at seventeen...")

Bullying is rampant in our society. In her book *Making a Bully-Free World*, author Pamela Hall states that "every seven minutes a child in the United States is bullied"[3] and "about 40 percent of kids have been bullied online."[4] Many bullies have left the playground, graduated from high school, and are now running companies, leading various levels of government, running for political office, hosting TV shows, and influencing society.

> "every seven minutes a child in the United States is bullied"
> –Pamela Hall

Sometimes I feel like Haley Joel Osment's character who "sees dead people" in the movie *The Sixth Sense*. I see bullies! Bullying is not part of my subconscious mind; it's become part of my conscious mind. I see bullies in places where others do not. I see bullies, and I hope after reading this book, you not only see them, but you join the revolution in stopping their destructive actions.

Lesson learned: Stand up to bullies!

Questions for reflection

1. What childhood bullies do you recall?
2. What, if any, labels did they stamp on you or others? How did it make you feel?
3. What individuals do you know who stood up to bullies? How did they do this? What impact did it have?
4. How would you go about standing up for someone you believe is being bullied?
5. Why is bullying so destructive?

2

"Sunday Morning Comin' Down"

Let me begin by stating that this chapter is not intended to be an indictment of the Catholic Church. When you read chapter 3, you will better understand this comment. I didn't plan to include this story in my book until I had a conversation with an acquaintance a few months ago. He is a practicing Catholic and wondered whether I was as well. I relayed a story to him about my first confession. I told him about the book I was writing, and he commented that he thought I had been bullied then, based on the story I shared with him.

My First Confession

I grew up in the Catholic Church, and while I went to public schools, my mother (who was Catholic) had an agreement with my father (who was Protestant) that we children would be raised Catholic. I believe that the actual agreement was that we would be raised as Catholics until we were "of age" to decide what direction our faith would take us. So, along with being baptized as infants, we all made our First Holy Communion (now called the Eucharist), our First Confession (now referred to as Reconciliation), and, except for my younger sister, our Confirmation in the Catholic Church.

It was kind of fun going to public school and being Catholic. We were excused from class every now and then to be given instruction at the church in preparation for making our First Confession. We had some final instruction for this, and then the big day finally arrived. I got to confess to the priest all the sins I'd committed thus far as a child, so that I could be forgiven. I remember walking into church that day. This church always seemed enormous to me as a child, yet it also felt holy to me. A life-size crucifix hung above the altar. A statue of the Blessed Mother and other statues stood around the perimeter of the sanctuary. There always seemed to be several candles lit. All of this created a very spiritual and hallowed kind of environment.

On the day of my First Confession, we were ushered to a section of the church that I'd never really noticed before. I remember being in awe of the confessional booths, which I had never noticed before either. They looked very sacred, and I knew that this would be a very special moment for me.

Little did I know that it would remain imprinted on my memory almost fifty years later. I watched some of my classmates go into one of the two confessional booths that were being used on this occasion. I remember looking up and noticing that a light came on outside of the booth to let others know when the confessional was occupied. It was very dark in the church, and to pass the time, I remember staring at the crucifix above the altar.

When it was my turn, I went into the confessional, closed the door, and knelt on the padded kneeler. I didn't realize at the time that the priest was now taking the confession of the person who was in the confessional on the other side of him. Okay, I got it. One priest was rotating back and forth between the two confessional booths. The only thing separating me from the priest was a very small window containing a screen, which was in the middle of the wall I was kneeling in front of. I wasn't sure if I was supposed to be praying or rehearsing the list of sins I'd been thinking about, so I remained very, very quiet.

Eventually, the window opened in front of me, and a small light was turned on. All I could see was a screen separating me from the priest and a light shining on my face. Then I whispered, "Bless me, Father, for I have sinned. This is my first confession." The priest was invisible to me. I noticed only a slight spec of light when I tried to peer through the screen.

Well, I got down to business quickly and rolled off every sin I had committed as far back as my memory would allow. When I was done, the priest told me what prayers to pray and how many times to pray them. My father was a very strict disciplinarian as well as an alcoholic, so I probably feared him more than I cared to admit. But on that day, I grew to fear the priest even more. I made the mistake of saying, "Yes, sir" when the priest finished giving me the penance for my sins.

I don't know that any other child in my group got to see what was present on the other side of the secret screen, but I sure did. Those innocent words had no sooner left my lips when the priest opened the screen, poked a very long finger in my face, and said, "Don't you ever refer to me as 'sir' again, young lady. You must only refer to me as 'Father.'"

Wow. Up to that point in my life, I don't think I had ever been dressed down by anyone like that—other than my highly autocratic father, and even he hadn't used that tone with me (yet). I remember standing up and almost instantaneously starting to cry. By the time I opened the door to walk out, I was sobbing. Did that just happen? Did the priest just yell at me during my First Confession?

I remember walking back to the pew that I had left, and as I knelt, the tears continued to stream down my face. I felt as though everyone in the church was staring at me, especially the statues. I wondered what my classmates were thinking.

What a terrible person I must be to be bawling my eyes out. I bet they were wondering what horrible sins I'd committed. I've talked to other Catholics as an adult, and I haven't found another person who felt under attack while making his or her First Confession.

Oddly enough, according to an article titled "The Seven Catholic Sacraments" on the website AmericanCatholic.org, the Catholic Sacrament of Reconciliation is supposed to lead us to God's unconditional forgiveness and to our need to forgive others. The Sacrament has three elements: conversion, confession, and celebration.[5] Clearly, I missed that. I wasn't celebrating in my heart, and I missed the feeling of complete forgiveness. I find a great deal of irony in that, given the struggles I've endured trying to forgive others.

Mother's Day

A year or so after making my First Confession, I remember sitting in that same church during a very crowded mass. It was Mother's Day, and it was so full that there was no room either in the crying room or balcony. (It was understood that if you had an infant, you were to listen to the mass from the crying room. If that was full, then you were relegated to the balcony.) In those years, the mass was still spoken in Latin. It was difficult for me to stay focused, because I had no idea what the priest was saying or chanting.

But at one point in the mass, the same priest who had heard my First Confession unexpectedly stopped the mass to chastise a young father who was seated in the church (and not in the crying room). The father was holding a newborn baby who was inconsolable. The priest demanded that the father either quiet the baby or leave the church. You could have heard a pin drop at that moment. The

> You see, I came to realize very young in life that bullies weren't just on playgrounds, in homerooms, or in history classes.

young father stood up and said, "Maybe you remember that today is Mother's Day, Father. And maybe you remember that Jesus said to love the little children?"

You see, I came to realize very young in life that bullies weren't just on playgrounds, in homerooms, or in history classes. Bullies were in churches too. But odd as it may seem, you'll learn later how the Catholic Church ultimately saved my life.

Lesson Learned: Bullying is wrong—no matter where it takes place!

Questions for reflection

1. What role, if any, does church play in your life?
2. What responsibility do churches have in the lives of those who seek their teachings?
3. Should bullies in churches be approached? Why or why not?
4. Have you ever been bullied in church? Have you shared your story with someone who can help? Why or why not?
5. What is the distinction between spiritual guidance and bullying?

3

"In My Room"

Escape

As one of seven children and one of only two girls in my family, I often shared a bedroom with my younger sister. I didn't mind, but I think she didn't always appreciate a bossy older sister invading her space. When I was thirteen, the only children still at home were my younger sister and a brother who was just two years older than I was. We each had our *own* rooms for the first time.

My bedroom was right next to my sister's bedroom, but on some days, I really envied hers. It had a nice, walk-in closet, an air conditioner (which I benefited from), and one very interesting feature: a fire escape allowed her passage to my brother's bedroom below in case a fire started on the second floor and she was unable to access the stairs. All she had to do was lift a panel in her floor and descend a wooden ladder that was built into the wall of my brother's bedroom. Forget the fire; if things got a little too tough, all she had to do was lift that panel and go hang out with our brother.

I, however, had a tremendous fear of heights, even as a child. Just the thought of descending that built-in vertical ladder gave me tremendous anxiety. My sister was brave, but I had too many self-inflicted fears that produced terror when I thought about needing to descend that ladder!

However, while my bedroom didn't have a cool (if scary) fire escape, it did house the gun cabinet, ammunition, and oh… the key to the gun cabinet. My sister and I both knew where the key was hidden. (I know, seriously?)

At thirteen, I thought that my life was horrible. I really didn't want to live. Some of that was due to the bullying I endured, and some was due to the abuse at home. (That's another book, but to this day, I remain grateful for my siblings.) I remember one day that summer, I kept banging my head against the headboard of my bed. Yes, I literally banged my head until it really began to hurt, and it occurred to me that I had an escape hatch too. Maybe I should just take out the .22-caliber rifle and shoot myself. I was good at target shooting. In fact, I once shot a bee while target shooting. Okay, to be fair, the bee *did* climb down the barrel of my rifle just as I was pulling the trigger. But still…it's a good story, isn't it?

I suppose I had a moment like George Bailey did in the film *It's a Wonderful Life*. While ending my life would end my suffering, who would take care of my sister? Even though to her, I had become the bossy big sister, I really worried about her. My parents had just divorced, and I was worried about a lot of things. Would our mom be okay? Would my sister be okay? The youngest of our older brothers was heading to college in just a couple of years, and my sister would be all by herself. I realized that I had to suck it up and get through it. You see, I hadn't even seen *It's a Wonderful Life* yet. I wasn't exposed to that movie until many years later. As I mentioned earlier, it was the Catholic Church that ultimately saved my life as a kid.

Yes, the same church that made my First Confession an embarrassing yet defining moment for me. Yes, the same church that was so rigid on Mother's Day that a young father was asked to leave the mass while trying to comfort his baby. Despite the autocratic and bullying leadership style of the priest who led that parish, the church instilled in me a deep faith in and fear of God. I remember praying on that day that he would help me, and indeed he did.

Looking back, had I taken my life, I would have missed out on so many marvelous things: my family; my college experiences; my wonderful, kind-hearted husband; and the many amazing friends and business acquaintances I've made. I'd like to think that like George Bailey, I may have even helped a few people along the way.

I realized that taking one's life is a shortsighted solution with dire consequences. You can't undo it. You can't imagine the pain, suffering, and despair that you create in the souls of those you leave behind. I realized that much later in life through knowing people who've lost loved ones to suicide. The scars don't heal easily. I also think that suicide is *not* a brave thing to do. My husband told me years ago that he wouldn't have had the courage to take his life. But I think it's more courageous to face the bully, face your fear, overcome your obstacles, and *live*. I believe that we are all created for a purpose. How can you ever fully discover and fulfill your purpose unless you have the *courage* to forge ahead? For this too shall pass.

The Facts

There are some undeniable, cold, hard facts about suicide. On its website, the American Foundation for Suicide Prevention[6] lists many health and environmental factors that may contribute to that decision. Some are obvious:

- depression
- bipolar disorder
- schizophrenia, etc.

What was alarming to me were some of the other factors. They include the following:

- access to lethal means (such as firearms)
- exposure to someone else's suicide
- prolonged stress factors such as harassment and bullying
- stressful events such as divorce or job loss
- previous suicide attempts by oneself or family members

My mom was bipolar and had attempted suicide a few times while still married to my father. I had access to firearms. At thirteen, I had been bullied most of my life. My parents had recently divorced. Check, check, check, and check.

I'm not so naïve as to think that my life was so different from those of many others. And the truth is, there is a great deal of information available to us today to help prevent suicide. The American Foundation for Suicide Prevention[7] lists many warning signs, a few of which include the following:

- someone talking about being a burden or not having a reason to live
- someone in unbearable physical pain
- someone exhibiting new or increased behavior
- increased use of drugs or alcohol
- acting recklessly
- sleeping too much or too little

- giving things away, saying good-bye
- signs of depression, anxiety, rage, or humiliation

A study of children who were bullied throughout adolescence revealed that they had high rates of depression and anxiety disorders. In addition, in a group that included both bullies and victims, the victims had the most adverse outcomes as young adults. Nearly 25 percent of this group reported having suicidal thoughts as adults.[8]

In 2014, the Center for Disease Control (CDC), in conjunction with the National Center for Injury Prevention and Control and the Division of Violence Protection, published a white paper titled, "The Relationship Between Bullying and Suicide: What We Know and What It Means for Schools." This study revealed that while it can't be stated definitively that bullying causes suicides, youth who have been involved in bullying behavior report higher levels of suicidal thoughts than youth who have not reported involvement in bullying behavior.[9] There is nothing healthy about being bullied. It is not a normal rite of passage for youth to endure. And for children who have other risk factors for suicide, the outcome can be devastating.

Parents, talk to your kids. Ask them how things are going at school. The CDC uses the term *protective factors* in reference to things that can mitigate suicide-related behavior. Does your child have a strong, positive connection to school? Does your child have a strong, positive connection to family and friends? These are simple questions, yet they can be lifesaving.

Shame, Shame, Shame

A friend of mine (who is a psychologist) recently shared with me that shame is one of the most harmful emotions we can experience. We often hide shame, and when we do so, it can weigh on us and have a negative impact on our health.[10] Shame is often a negative emotion that follows another negative emotion. For those who have been bullied, the hurtful words and actions are bad enough. They, in and of themselves, can cause serious emotional distress. Then it starts to sink in, and you think, I must really be a loser because *I'm* the target of their bullying.

Looking back, that's exactly how I felt in school. I didn't share my bullying (or harassment) with anyone because I was ashamed. I felt as though I must deserve that treatment because I really was unworthy of being treated like a normal kid.

Later, as an adult, there were two situations in two different organizations when I did tell someone in leadership about bullying. Those leaders did very little (in one case, absolutely nothing) to investigate my claims. In one instance, I confided to another female who could have and should have done something. After each of those experiences, it took time for me to rid myself of the self-loathing that was all too reminiscent of my teenage years.

Human Resources

It's time for leaders and human-resource professionals to step it up. I address legislation against bullying in appendix E. Regardless of whether there are state or federal laws enacted when you read this, bullying is not healthy, and to allow it in a workplace really makes a statement about a company's values and culture. Leaders who bully are at the lowest level imaginable on the leadership food chain. Yes, they may get results, incredible results. But at what cost? *Profit* is not a dirty word unless it comes at the expense of treating people with dignity and respect.

> **Profit is not a dirty word unless it comes at the expense of treating people with dignity and respect.**

While workplace bullying may involve yelling and public humiliation, it often is much more insidious. It may occur in a private meeting with no other witnesses. It may include excessive criticism, intimidation, or singling out someone; in my case, it was a leader who looked me in the eye and lied about his bullying when I confronted him. I hope you never encounter the narcissist bully or the narcissistic sociopathic bully. Their methods are even more sinister.

Lesson learned: Live so you can fulfill your life's purpose!

Questions for Reflection

1. What bullies have you faced in your life?
2. How have you overcome their abuse?
3. Have you ever heard anyone state that he or she would be better off dead? What, if anything, did you do? What could you have done?
4. What is your purpose? What is it that's unique or special about you?
5. How can you help (yourself or someone else) increase positive connectedness to school and to family and friends?

4

"Wooly Bully"

College Days

I longed for college as a new experience. Only two other people in my high-school class had applied to the school that I chose, so I thought I would finally be able to leave behind the misery of high school as well as my August anxiety. August isn't a person; it's not a bully's name. I am referring to the calendar month. In fact, I almost titled this book *Hating August*.

You see, I grew to hate August because it was a reminder that September—when the bullying would start up all over again—was only a few weeks away. I know God must have a sense of humor because my birthday is in August! Thankfully, I grew to almost like August—but only after I'd left high school far, far behind.

I belonged to a Methodist youth group during my junior and senior years of high school, and in it, I experienced real friendships for the first time. I couldn't believe that this group of kids didn't care how much I weighed, how I wore my hair, or that I had worn thick glasses in my freshman year. And I can tell you that they never pressed me about whether I was a Christian. They loved me anyway!

I was so excited when I was accepted to Grove City College, located north of Pittsburgh in Grove City, Pennsylvania. Little did I know what a profound impact this small liberal-arts college would have on my life. When I started college, I knew that I believed in God, but that was it. I feared God and respected God, but I can't say that I loved God. And what did Jesus have to do with anything? God allowed me to be tormented for my *entire* childhood, didn't he? In fact, I only applied to Grove City College because it was affordable. I had my sights set on Hawaii or Colorado.

My father had remarried (see chapter 9), and I wanted to get as far away from my new stepmother as possible. But the reality was, I hadn't applied for any scholarships, and I couldn't afford to attend college out of state. That was lucky for me, because Grove City College ultimately changed my life, although I learned some difficult lessons there too.

Grove City provided the same sense of comfort that my high-school youth group gave me. I remember feeling a little anxious about what it would be like to start over, and I discovered that it was an incredible new opportunity. By my sophomore year, I had blossomed. I got contact lenses, cut my hair, and started buying more stylish clothes (instead of making my own). I felt confident for perhaps the first time in my life. I was being asked out on dates, and a sorority or two even invited me to rush. I was working out on a regular basis and still trying to jog outdoors (though I was advised by one of the coaches to walk instead of run).

During my sophomore year, I became a good friend of a guy I'll call Jake. Jake was someone I would run into in the library. We were supposed to study in the library (I know, what a revelation). But it became the place to see and to be seen. People connected and met up in the library. Guys asked girls out in the library. And, I soon learned, friends set you straight in the library.

I Think I'm Funny

I had developed a bad habit of using my razor-sharp tongue. I took considerable pride in being quick witted. I had a comeback for anything that anyone said, and it didn't matter how rude or hurtful it was. I thought that this was my God-given gift—my unique talent!

I remember sitting in the college chapel one day, waiting for the service to begin. In walked a few guys who sat right in front of my friends and me. I had dated one of them. We had only gone out a few times, and I didn't want to date him more than that. He was a very nice guy and very kind, but I didn't want to have a serious boyfriend. I wanted to experience what had been denied to me in high school. I wanted to date around and experience a variety of different relationships.

In hindsight, I'm sure I must have hurt this guy in some way when I turned him down after a few dates, but that was never my intention. On this day, he turned around and started a conversation with me. I don't remember what we discussed, but I do remember that at one point, he said, "You know, Mary, I'm not as dumb as I look."

Without missing a beat, I said, "I know; you couldn't possibly be."

My friends who were sitting with me kind of chuckled, but this guy and his fraternity brothers didn't find any humor in my quick retort. Neither did my friend, Jake.

A few days later, I was back in the library, seeking a book that I needed to read for a paper I was writing. Jake saw me and came over. Like everyone else in the library, we started talking. I always joked with Jake, and he usually laughed at my warped sense of humor. That day, he didn't laugh. Instead, he said, "You think you're really funny and quick witted, but sometimes you say things that are really hurtful to others, and it's not funny when you hurt other people."

Yikes, I thought. Jake was right. I thought I was beginning to become popular because I was the funny girl. Instead, I was doing a little bullying of my own, and Jake had the courage to let me know. I began to wonder how many other bullies had previously been bullied.

The CDC refers to this group as bully-victims. What I didn't realize is that bully-victims (those who have been bullied and subsequently bully others) are at an even greater risk than others are for depression, anxiety, and suicidal thoughts.[11]

> What I didn't realize is that bully-victims (those who have been bullied and subsequently bully others) are at an even greater risk than others for depression, anxiety, and suicidal thoughts.

I lost touch with Jake after college. That was undoubtedly my fault. Although we were living in different states, I tried to connect with him on LinkedIn a few years ago. Turns out Jake and I had a couple of connections in common in our LinkedIn networks. Even so, I never got a response from Jake, which made me a little sad. You see, I wanted to express my gratitude, which I should have done in 1979 or 1980. I wanted to tell him how much I appreciated his friendship back then and apologize for my sharp tongue. I also wanted to thank him for having the courage to stand up to me and hold me accountable. I'm not sure how many other friends would have taken that chance, but I'm grateful that *he* did.

I wish all bullies had someone like Jake in their lives—someone who would put the brakes on and tell them enough is enough, someone who would risk losing a friend to do the right thing. I believe that Jake is somewhere in the Virginia/Washington, DC, area. I hope that someday he knows what a profound impact he had on me at that tiny little college in Northwestern Pennsylvania.

Lesson learned: Bullying others is never okay, even if you've been bullied.

Questions for Reflection

1. Do you know any bully-victims?
2. How can you help them?
3. Have you ever bullied anyone?
4. If so, looking back, what type of impact do you believe this had on the person you bullied?
5. How can you make amends?

PART II
Victim to Victor

5

"Mean Girls"

Band Geek

There was a tremendous amount of peer pressure when I was in high school, and I think it's even more pronounced today. If you were raised by good parents, believe them when they tell you that you are a wonderful person and you don't need to follow the crowd. If you are a parent, I hope you can instill this in your children.

Whether you are an athlete, a musician, a math and science whiz, or an artist, it doesn't matter. Be true to your authentic self, and choose your friends wisely. It used to bother me to see how many "friends" some of the popular kids in high school had. I probably only had a handful of friends. I thought I must have been tough on my friends because I had so few, but in hindsight, I made the right choices.

Several people claimed to be my friends, but they were "mean girls." They would pretend to be nice to me and then gossip about me behind my back. I was in the band in high school, and by sophomore year, I had moved up from the second flute section to fourth chair in the first flute section. My friend (I'll call her Sally), also a flutist, was genuinely happy for me. She remained far down the line in the second flute section, where I used to sit, but she didn't care. We weren't competing with each other. She was my friend.

Some of the other flutists were upset. You see, they seemed to think I belonged in the second flute section, where I previously was relegated. What they failed to understand was that it was my tenacity in practicing, practicing, practicing that helped me to advance. Eventually, I was moved to second chair in symphonic band and first chair in the marching band. Again, to my face, many of the popular girls in the section smiled and talked to me. Behind my back, though, they questioned why I had moved up. In their narrow minds, I really wasn't a very good flutist.

Well, I *was* that good because I practiced for hours every week. Music was my salvation. I could get lost in my practicing and block out the dysfunction that was my family.

I wasn't a naturally gifted musician. I didn't play piano or guitar. Playing an instrument didn't come easily for me. Every time our band director went down the line in our section and made us play by ourselves in front of the entire band, I was ready. In freshman year, I was embarrassed when he did this, which is why he started me far back in the second flute section. I vowed that I would never play that poorly again. That was a defining moment for me.

By the way, you're not a bad parent if your child isn't first or second chair in band. And you're not a loser if you were never first or second chair in band. I had no other real hobbies, and I desperately needed an escape in high school. Lucky for me, I'd started playing the flute in elementary school. I never cared about being a good flute player until I was in high school. I realized then that I needed to feel good about something, since some of my classmates were only too eager to make me feel badly about myself.

I ultimately chose not to hang around with the mean girls. Eventually, I didn't really care about their gossiping. I focused on the couple of close friends I had, and that was enough. For me, it wasn't about the number of friends I had; it was about the *quality* of the friendships I had.

If I'm being honest, I probably had fewer than five trustworthy friends in high school. And sadly, my very best friend, Linda, moved away before high school. She was Chinese and wore glasses about as thick as mine were. I think we became such good friends because the rest of the world decided that we looked different and that we must be nerds because we were both scholars. We liked to study. We excelled in our classes.

I've dropped many friends over the years because they sucked the energy right out of me. They didn't add any value to my life, and the friendships felt like one-way relationships. Friendships cannot be one way, and you can't continue to break someone's trust and remain a good friend. By the way, don't let this section title fool you. Boys can be just as mean and bully just as much as "mean girls" do.

If people stab you in the back, they are *not* your friends. Don't let them get to you. I can promise you that this behavior will catch up with them later in life and will absolutely hinder their ability to function in healthy corporate cultures. No one has the right to take away anybody's self-esteem (or attempt to do so). When you come across people who do that, choose to love them anyway, but don't spend your precious time with them. If you do, your emotional gas tank will become depleted. Instead, find a few close friends who will accept you for who you are.

> **No one has the right to take away anybody's self-esteem (or attempt to do so).**

Be Social without Media

Speaking of dropping things, consider how much time you spend and what you are revealing on social media. Talk about a forum for bullying! I laugh every time someone reminds me of Eleanor Roosevelt's quote about self-esteem: "No one can make you feel inferior without your consent." I beg to differ. Bullies naturally pick on others who lack self-esteem. It's what they do. I'm sure many other victims would agree that Eleanor didn't get that one quite right.

Eleanor also wasn't dealing with the world of the Internet and social media. I wrote a song a couple of years ago about social media. You'll find it at the end of this chapter. I hesitated to add it, but the fact is, our children spend so much time texting, tweeting, and posting that many of them have very poorly developed social skills. Communication skills, confrontation skills, and coping skills seem to have become lost arts.

People are duped all the time on social websites and dating websites. When I talk about having a few close friends who accept you for who you are, I'm talking about people whom you truly know and who know you. You've met them face-to-face. You've had a meal with them; you've shared dreams and frustrations, and your confidence has not been broken. You've challenged them respectfully or disagreed with them, and you're still friends.

I think it's great to have global connections and friendships (we used to call them pen pals). Just remember that the data you share doesn't ever go away, and you may not want it forwarded or posted elsewhere—which can happen when people are not really your friends.

By the way, if you or someone you know is ever bullied on social media, you will be better able to cope if you know how to communicate with your parents or your loved ones. That's another reason to learn how to have a little ol' conversation!

Are You My Friend?

So, who are you spending your time with? Do your friends lift you up or push you down? Why would you ever spend time with friends who don't lift you up? Again, I'm going to assume that if you are reading this book, you are a teenager or an adult. At some point as a teen, you can use judgment to make choices about how you spend your time and with whom. One of my favorite quotes is by the late author and speaker Jim Rohn, who said, "You are the average of the five people you spend the most time with."

Make the right choices. It can lead to a much more fulfilling life. I am no longer upset that I still have only a few very close friends. The people to whom I've assigned that title love me unconditionally. They've seen the good, the bad, and the ugly sides of me, and they love what's in my core.

Even in my middle age, I've chosen to let some friendships fade into the sunset because they were not uplifting or fulfilling. And I'm okay with that. I've also chosen not to attend any more of my high-school reunions (having only attended one). Why would I want to spend an evening with people whom I really didn't know and who never knew me? I learned an important principle about time last year. You really can't manage time, but you can choose how you spend it and how you place value on it. I hope you value your time too and choose to spend it in a way that is encouraging and with those who are inspiring and uplifting to you.

A Little Ol' Conversation (My Original Song)

I recently found myself alone.
Somethin' fairly new to me.
A friend of mine said, "Don't worry, babe."
Datin's not like it used to be.
You just go online and lie about yourself,
'Cuz everyone else does too.
You don't really meet; you just chat and tweet,
And virtualize yourself 'til you're through.

Chorus:
That's why I'm not your Facebook friend, your hashtag Tweet,

And I don't wanna LinkIn with you.
I wanna sit right down and look ya in the eye,
So, I'll tell ya what I'm gonna do.
I ain't gonna text, or blog, or chat,
'Cuz it only causes me frustration.
So, give your thumbs a rest, your vocal chords a test;
Could we just have a little conversation?

And you can be a star on YouTube;
Ya get your fifteen minutes of fame.
Well, pardon me, if I don't post,
'Cuz that fifteen minutes is lame.
Whatever happened to common sense?
Am I the only one who sees?
It don't go away, and it'll ruin your day
Until you're 'bout a hundred and three.
(Repeat Chorus)

Bridge
Well, back at work I gotta tell ya
Things are not really the same.
We forgot how to walk, converse, and talk,
'Cuz e-mail's the name of the game.
Can you imagine a world where we don't speak,
'Cuz we're networked clear to Timbuktu?
Well, call me crazy, but we've gotten lazy,
Pushin' buttons is all that we do…

(Repeat Chorus)

Ending
I wanna real-life conversation. Not LOL OMG!

Lesson learned: You are stronger than you think!

Questions for Reflection

1. What friendships do you need to let go of?
2. How much time do you spend on social media (or how much time do your children spend on social media)?
3. What kind of information do you read/post on social media?
4. How effectively can you communicate your opinion when others disagree with you?
5. Do others retreat or silence themselves when you disagree with them? How can you help them become better at developing communication and confrontation skills?

6

"You've Got a Friend"

It's Not about Me

If you've been cyberbullied or otherwise demeaned, one of the best ways to start feeling better about yourself is to focus on being kind to others or showing genuine appreciation toward them. In other words, put your focus on other people and not on yourself. You will be amazed at how much better you'll feel. Kindness can be extended in a variety of ways. Nonprofits are always looking for financial help and free labor. If you don't have the financial means, volunteer your time at a food bank or a soup kitchen. You will see others who have struggled in ways you can't imagine. When you are kind and help others, you feel better yourself. You boost the levels of serotonin and endorphins in your brain!

Since this book is about bullying, do something unexpected and kind for someone who has been bullied at school, at work, anywhere. You have no idea what kind of an impact one simple kind gesture can have.

And speaking of kind gestures, why not visit an elderly or ailing relative? I recently heard someone say, "The most important years of your life are the year you come into this world and the year you leave." Go to a nursing home. It's a blessing for residents to have visitors. As one who had a loved one in a nursing home (before moving her back in with us), I was sad to see that most residents get very few visitors. Staff can direct you to those who would benefit from a visit and who would enjoy your company. It's easy to forget your sorrows when you are in the moment and focusing on someone else.

> "The most important years of your life are the year you come into this world and the year you leave."

Depending upon your age, you can deliver Meals on Wheels or help Habitat for Humanity build houses. During the holidays, or any time of the year, you can help bake cookies for men and women in the military overseas.

As ridiculous as this sounds, try not to be rude to the next telemarketer who calls. You have no idea what is going on in *his* or *her* life. Maybe that's the only job he or she had the courage to take or the job he or she needs to pay the bills. You can just take a moment and listen; you don't have to buy what that person is selling, but you *can* treat him or her with dignity. Telemarketers are, after all, human, just like you and me—unless it's an automated computer call, in which case, feel free to hang up!

I must admit that I haven't always practiced this. But my husband and I made a vow recently to either let the phone ring and allow the call to go to voice mail or answer it and be polite. If we can't be polite, then we don't answer the phone. We have no right to ruin someone else's day or demean someone because we are stressed. (We use voice mail a lot!)

Tough Love Is Tough

There are even extreme cases that involve helping others through something called tough love. Regrettably, I have too many examples that involve coworkers being under the influence at work.

Two similar situations involved people who failed drug tests. In both situations, the companies had policies that were clear about prohibiting employees from using drugs or alcohol at work or being under the influence.

In both situations, the team members tested positive for illegal substances. In one situation, I had to fire someone I considered to be a friend. It was one of the worst days of my professional career.

There were no signs of erratic behavior. He simply made the mistake of telling the wrong person that he liked to smoke pot on the weekends. When I confronted him, he denied smoking pot. I explained that he would have to take a drug test. He still denied using drugs.

I tried to advocate for him, but the decision maker in this company was inflexible. If the employee tested positive, I had to fire him. This young man didn't report to me, which made it even more awkward.

When the positive test came back, I tried to encourage my coworker to stop smoking pot, as he would have difficulty passing a drug test when interviewing elsewhere. He was furious with me. I reminded him that he, not I, had made the decision to smoke pot and tell others about it. I never heard from him again, but I hope by now he understands that he was responsible for his termination.

I had another very different situation involving drug use. In this instance, another coworker admitted using drugs when it became apparent that I needed to have him take a drug test.

This guy was furious with me and told me that he felt bullied. I looked him straight in the eye and told him that I wasn't going to go home that night knowing that he could potentially have an accident at work and hurt himself or someone else—or have an accident on his way home that night. He was going to take a drug test, or I would have to exercise our company's policy and terminate his employment. My tone of voice was compassionate; I was not the HR police playing "gotcha."

He then told me that he would take the drug test (his supervisor agreed to drive him to the facility), though he was sure he was going to test positive. I told him that we should take it a step at a time. I could tell he was *really* upset, and I didn't want him leaving my office in despair. I explained that even if he did test positive, he had the option of entering a drug-rehabilitation program and that if he did that, he would not be fired. I explained that the choice was ultimately his, but we needed to take it a step at a time.

He failed the drug test just as he'd predicted; however, he checked himself into a wonderful rehabilitation program. This program was tough and demanded far more from him than what we required of employees in this situation. He chose to keep in touch with me, and I enjoyed hearing from him. It gave me an opportunity to listen to him genuinely and offer encouragement.

In fact, something remarkable happened during his stay in rehab. He sent me a very lengthy e-mail, which I've kept to this day. He told me about his struggles with addiction and said that I "probably saved his life" by sending him to take the drug test. I remember reading that sentence and becoming more than a little choked up. I remember reading his e-mail late one night and wiping a few tears from my tired eyes. I'm not sure he knows how much that e-mail has meant to me and how much I appreciated his recognition that tough love is not the same as bullying.

I've also had to have some pretty direct conversations with employees accused of sexual harassment. One situation involved a few people who admitted to the behavior that they were accused of; however, they could not have cared less.

In fact, one of them ultimately tried to get me fired because he thought that the situation I was investigating was none of my business. I think he was more than a little surprised when I stood my ground and completed the investigation. Ultimately, he, not I, left the company.

I'm an advocate and a reseller of a preemployment screening profile called ZeroRisk HR Employment Assessment. This profile reveals how each of us is hardwired and helps companies identify, hire, and retain top talent.[12]

I have found it to be invaluable not only for making better hiring decisions but also in helping with personal development and team building. Because of the way I'm wired, I am balanced in an "emotional intelligence" or EQ facet called "intuition and empathy." If you are balanced in this facet, you can be incredibly kind, compassionate, and caring. However, you are also capable of holding others completely accountable when they cross the line. I personally have no problem being direct, blunt, and holding others accountable.

As odd as it may seem, I believe that I was being kind by holding my coworkers accountable. You probably have been angry with good friends from time to time because they have held you accountable for something.

> The difference between accountability and bullying is evidenced in our choice of words, our tone of voice, our body language, and our intentions.

The difference between accountability and bullying is evidenced in our choice of words, our tone of voice, our body language, and our intentions.

An Attitude of Gratitude

I've also learned to express gratitude to those who have shown true friendship by holding me accountable or showing me great kindness. This year, I've decided to send a note of gratitude or thanks to someone every week. I know that may sound kind of silly, but it's so inspiring to create surprise and delight by letting others know how much you appreciate them.

I recently sent a note of thanks to a special florist in Columbus, Ohio. This action was directly related to a separate note of gratitude I had sent to a dear friend of my husband and me, Jo. She and her husband, Bob, had come to our annual New Years' Day brunch. This was probably not my most well-thought-out annual celebration, but I had committed to doing it, and by golly, I wasn't going to let my friends and family down. They'd come to look forward to it. Let me just say that if you decide to do a New Year's Day brunch, you'll be watching the ball in Time's Square drop on TV while you're drinking way too many caffeinated beverages to stay awake and finish your food preparation!

That year, I was not feeling well the week prior to our New Year's Day brunch. I had gone to a local pharmacy clinic to be sure I didn't have strep throat. Nope. I had "the crud" that was going around. It was viral, and I was informed there was no medicine I could take to eradicate it. I debated canceling the brunch, but I started feeling better two days before New Year's Day. I decided the worst was behind me, and I could toughen up and do this!

The truth is that I had no energy. By the time New Year's Day came, I was at least an hour behind in food preparation. Jo and her husband were the first to arrive, and Jo (who had previously owned a bed-and-breakfast with Bob) knew just what to do. She didn't ask for directions, and she wisely ignored my responses to her question, "Anything I can do to help?" (I'm stubborn by nature, so it's difficult for me to accept help. But I welcomed Jo's assistance on that day and was deeply grateful.)

Besides wanting to show my appreciation, I also knew that Jo planned to retire the following week. So, I sent an arrangement of flowers to her from a florist I'd found to be simply the best, as its arrangements are exquisite and affordable. I sent Jo one of the shop's daily specials, and much to my delight, she called me the day it was delivered and raved about how beautiful it was. That gave me a chance to express my gratitude again for all that she did to rescue me at the brunch.

So, my letter of gratitude to this florist was to thank the staff for creating such beautiful arrangements. Everyone who has ever received flowers from me has raved about how beautiful they are. I am grateful, too, that the florist offers arrangements that are not only beautiful but also affordable. I'm on a tight budget right now as I attempt to launch my own business, and this florist made it possible for me to send a dear friend a token of thanks without breaking the bank.

Gratitude can take the form of an e-mail or a simple phone call too. It really doesn't have to cost anything. You will find that this kindness is contagious. You will spread joy that others will in turn spread to others.

I also recently located a former supervisor of mine (from thirty years ago) on LinkedIn. His name was Warren, and he was one of the best leaders I'd ever worked for in my life. Once I found him on LinkedIn and connected, I wrote him a note of gratitude. He replied that my note was perhaps the kindest e-mail he'd ever received.

Bottom line: take the focus off yourself. I know it sounds easier than it really is, especially if you are actively being bullied; but it will feed your soul and help you to put things into perspective. As my husband once told me, being nice or being kind is free. It doesn't cost you anything, and it sure makes you feel good about yourself!

Lastly, consider keeping a gratitude journal. I used the following inspirational quote in a training session that I recently facilitated: "What if you woke up tomorrow with only the things you were grateful for today?"

While I've been unable to find the originator of this beautiful message, I've noticed that many people have posted it on their sites or blogs—understandable; it's compelling! We really do have much to be grateful for. Yes, even those of us who've been bullied!

Lesson learned: Take the focus off yourself, and focus on really helping someone else.

Questions for Reflection

1. To whom could you express gratitude? How can you do this?

2. What are you grateful for? Do you keep a gratitude journal?

3. If you woke up tomorrow morning with only those things you had expressed gratitude for today, how rich would your life be?

4. Who has shown you kindness or expressed gratitude toward you? How did it make you feel?

5. There's an old saying: "If you want to have a friend, you need to be a friend." What can you do to be a friend to others?

7

"Voices"

Gotta Sing

You may or may not know your Myers-Briggs personality type, but I bet I'm more introverted than you are. If I respond to the self-selecting statements honestly, I can score maybe two points in extroversion. Yes, that's the truth. I'm sure that part of this is due to my genetic makeup, as neither of my parents was particularly extroverted. I guess that my dysfunctional childhood had some influence on that too.

Early in my professional career, I realized that I needed to work on overcoming the self-loathing that had become part of my subconscious mind. Again, years of being told that I was fat and ugly were still taking a toll on me.

My second job out of college was with a wonderful restaurant chain. In its heyday, it had five hundred restaurants scattered across the United States. Because the chain was growing by leaps and bounds at one point, I was able to move up

"Voices"

pretty quickly. Soon, I found myself teaching training classes and moving into management and leadership roles within the organization.

I remember the paralyzing fear that swept over me anytime I had to speak to an audience. I'd usually settle in after about ten minutes, but boy, that first ten minutes was torture. I was allowing the voice in my head to become my own bully.

I'm a brooder and a thinker, and I began to wonder what was more terrifying to me than public speaking was. You've probably heard it said that studies have shown most people have a greater fear of public speaking than of death or dying. I knew I wasn't alone, but I also knew that I didn't want to spend quality time in the bathroom prior to speaking to a group. I had other fears, but I couldn't envision how conquering those might help me overcome my fear of public speaking.

Then it occurred to me. I was a musician in high school. I played the flute and piccolo. I had always wanted to be in the choir and be in musicals, but I was too nervous to try out. I never sang outside the safety of my shower or my bedroom.

I did a little shower singing in college and got busted one day. One of my floor mates heard me singing in the shower and waited for me to emerge from the bathroom. When I opened the door into the hallway, she cornered me and asked why I didn't join the college choir. She told me I had a great voice. Her name was Marilyn, and I will always remember how encouraging and sweet she was to me. Despite my gratitude for her kind words, however, I did nothing.

When I turned thirty, I decided to give myself the gift of voice lessons. I had just married my husband, and he had commented on what a great voice I had as I harmonized with anybody and everybody on the radio.

Well, one thing led to another. Four voice coaches later, I started to sing locally. I'm embarrassed to admit that two of my voice coaches fired me. Yep, talk about a kick to the old ego; however, both told me that I had a soloist's voice and that I needed to put myself out there and sing. If I didn't, they saw no need to continue voice lessons. By the way, they didn't bully me. They actually cared about me enough to try to help me overcome my self-loathing and self-doubt. It didn't work at first, but deep down, I knew they were right.

What they didn't realize, though, is that my motivation for taking voice lessons wasn't to become a singer. I was taking voice lessons to overcome my fear of public speaking. Along the way, I met John, a dear friend with a beautiful tenor voice who encouraged me to join a music ministry affiliated with his church. I remember the first gig I did with John. He invited me to join him at his annual Christmas concert. I practiced for hours for my big debut. Then the magical night was upon me.

I got to the church an hour early, so I could walk in and begin my visualization process. I walked up to the altar, turned around, and looked out into the sanctuary, imagining seeing the smiling faces of the congregation and visitors as they enjoyed the beautiful holiday music.

My visualization exercise quickly came to a halt when John arrived. We moved into vocal warm-up mode in the choir room, which was in the basement of the church. By the time we went upstairs, the crowd was beginning to gather. I could feel myself becoming a bit anxious and nervous, so I told John that I was going to sit in the sanctuary. He had reserved the first row of pews on each side of the aisle, and I grabbed my spot. I sat there quietly, praying that I would be able to sing when it was my turn to join John.

The concert began, and John and the other vocalists were quite good. I glanced at the program at one point and realized that there were only three songs left before I was to join John for the last two songs of the concert. The voice in my head kicked in, saying, "You're not really as good as the singers who've sung before you. What made you think you could really do this? If you think you're nervous now, just wait until you get up and see how many people have filled this church."

I hadn't even noticed the family that sat down with me in that front pew. However, at one point, my knees began shaking so badly that I kicked the person sitting next to me, who just happened to be David, the pastor of the church. To make matters worse, David was holding his newborn daughter, Jordan. Still, I knew that if I could get through the song I was about to sing with John, public speaking would be a walk in the park.

While I would never say that this concert was my best vocal performance or even a *very good* vocal performance, when it was over, I was proud that I had done it. I felt a huge sense of "being in control." I, with very little experience singing, got up and sang in front of a few hundred people. I didn't faint; I didn't have a heart attack. I was nervous, but I worked through it. I *had been* in control, despite the voice of doubt blasting in my head. I accomplished something challenging. And I achieved my initial goal. I broke through.

Not only did public speaking become easier, but I started teaching others how to become effective public speakers. I even started coaching executives on how to deliver dynamic presentations. I am still highly introverted, but I've learned how to make accommodation for that by overcoming my fear of public speaking and controlling the voice in my head.

Group Sing

I've said this in front of many classes, but one of the best ways to lessen your fear of public speaking (aside from the most beneficial practice of rehearse, rehearse, rehearse) is to go sing karaoke with your friends. Even if you get up with a group, there is something about singing that makes public speaking much less terrifying.

The next time you get up to speak, give yourself a little positive self-talk. "Hey, you got up Saturday night and sang 'All the Single Ladies.' If you can sing, you can speak." Singing is so much more personal and intimidating. Public speaking by comparison is so much easier.

Conquering the voice in your head will be just as empowering and freeing for you as it was for me. You will attain a positive self-image that most bullies can't begin to imagine. By the way, if you conquer your fear of public speaking, you will acquire a skill that will benefit you in almost anything you do. If you are still in high school, you probably have public-speaking classes or a debate team. That's a great place to start!

Remember, most people aren't wired to gravitate toward public speaking. Just look at the membership numbers of the Toastmaster organization! It has more than 332,000 members in more than 15,400 clubs in over 130 countries![13] You'll probably find others who will need your encouragement and who will encourage you! It could be a real game changer, and you deserve the chance to change your game!

Speaking of a game changer, having effective communication skills happens to be a big one! I don't mean to be critical of any generation, but you know how I feel about social media. Social media has become a huge weapon for bullies. It's also become a primary communication tool for generation Y (millennials) and generation Z.

Learning how to push a noun against a verb verbally could really help you compete in the workforce. Too many hide behind the one dimension of social media. It can be a little unsettling to have to look someone in the eye and have a tough conversation, but you will grow by leaps and bounds each time you do this.

Don't Bully the Bully

If you are being bullied on social media, tell someone who can help you. No matter what it is, don't allow anyone to demean or belittle you. We've all made horrendous mistakes and done things that in the moment don't seem surmountable. But we can pick ourselves up. *You* can pick yourself up. Besides, do you know that even bullies do things that cause them embarrassment? Of course, they do. They're human just

> "An eye for an eye makes the whole world blind." –Mahatma Gandhi

like you and I are. Don't match bully behavior with bully behavior. As Mahatma Gandhi once said, "An eye for an eye makes the whole world blind." The brave thing to do is to forgive and not fight back.

Bullies are trying to demean you and get you to respond emotionally. Surprise them and don't. Stop reading Twitter or participating in Facebook or YouTube if something was purposefully posted there to slander, upset, or bother you.

You are in control of the voice in your head. When the voices of self-doubt and low self-esteem show up at the door in your head…don't let them in. Bullies are like predators. They sense and seek out weaknesses in others. Confidence dispels weakness.

You are a worthy, special, and unique person. God created you to be just who you are—no more, no less. Can you imagine how boring the world would be if all the animals in the animal kingdom looked the same? Or if all the trees or plants in nature looked the same? Or if all birds chirped the same way? You are different from me, and that's the way it's supposed to be. If someone doesn't like you or me…that's *his or her* problem. The world is full of haters. The best weapon to use against them is *love*!

Lesson learned: Control the voice in your head. Reprogram it if necessary!

Questions for Reflection

1. What fears are holding you back?
2. How can you overcome them?
3. Who can help you?
4. What other resources do you have?
5. What other resources do you need?

8

"Help!"

Talk It Out

It doesn't matter if you are still in high school, in college, or somewhere on the journey of life after school. There are professionals whose purpose is to help others. If you work for a company, you may have a free Employee Assistance Plan. Some health-insurance plans also offer psychological counseling.

If you are in high school, talk to your parents, a school counselor, or an adult whom you trust. Don't keep your feelings inside and play the shame game. It's not about you. Bullying is about someone else's need to feel superior, and there are adults who want to and are poised to help.

If you are at college, you should contact someone in student affairs or a professor whom you trust. Undoubtedly, your college has services that can help you. Many counties also have free counseling services, which you can usually find on the Internet.

If you are a member of a religious group, talk to your pastor, priest, or rabbi. Many men and women of the clergy are helpful or can lead you to others in the church or community who can help you.

I talked to my first therapist in my middle age. After doing so, I realized that I should have sought counseling thirty years ago and really needed it forty years ago. I was kind of angry at myself. I was too proud to seek help because I thought I could handle my own problems. After all, I survived bullying, an alcoholic parent, a manic-depressive parent, molestation, inappropriate contact by a classmate in high school, sexual harassment at work, contemplation of suicide, and more. Hey, I didn't need any help; I was the survivor. I was the one who helped others.

Nevertheless, at one time, I'd left a job, and I was still angry weeks later. I was not at all happy with my former boss. I decided that maybe I needed to talk to someone. Maybe there *was* something wrong with me. Maybe I was sending out a weird vibe and didn't know it. Maybe my boss was right, and I wasn't as good in my job as I thought I'd been. Maybe I was struggling with depression.

My boss wanted me to indulge his ego each day at work. Clearly, I wasn't as overenthusiastic and extroverted in my leadership approach as he was. He was convinced he was perfect and everyone else needed to be as well. He seemed to be unaware that he came across to others and to me as incredibly fake. To make matters worse, he was put on a pedestal. It was as though his leadership style was revered by *his* boss. So, maybe there *was* something wrong with me because I couldn't fake it, or I *wouldn't* fake it.

Before leaving that job, I elected to begin Employee Assistance Program (EAP) counseling with a therapist whom I'll call Leslie. During my first session with Leslie, I completed a mound of paper work, which provided a family history for her to review. That was the toughest hour of my life. I had to talk about things that I hadn't discussed in quite some time—or *ever*.

Leslie really wanted to focus on the molestation I endured as a child, my alcoholic father, and my mentally ill mother. I didn't want to focus on that. I wanted her to tell me that my boss was a narcissistic sociopath and be done with it. Eventually, we got there, and she was very affirming in the steps I was planning to take.

While she never referred to my boss as a narcissistic sociopath, she agreed, based on my description, that I'd made the right decision to leave that company and that it was brave of me to do so. She also affirmed my belief that my boss probably was a bully.

During our sessions, she talked about the scars I had from childhood. I told her that I truly had forgiven my bullies, harassers, and parents many years ago. If I hadn't, I'm not sure I would have survived life. I told her that I'd realized years ago that holding on to hatred is wrong and self-destructive. Again, I credit my years at Grove City College for helping me to get on the right track. I'm not sure I would have had the career and the successes in life that I have enjoyed without the confidence and character that I developed at college.

As I've suggested, sometimes your true friends can point out your destructive tendencies. I am forever grateful to those who have helped me that way. However, I realize that if I had sought professional help sooner, my earlier life might have been more rewarding. At least I did seek professional help eventually, and it did make a difference. It helped me to realize that I am responsible for myself and that despite other people's actions against me, *I* make the choice; *I* choose my attitude.

I'm in Charge of Me!

I also came to realize that as a child, I could not control the bullies, the molesters, or the abusers. I have no idea why I had to go through some truly horrible things in my life. I do believe there is a reason for it; the very fact that I desire to help other victims of bullying may be the answer. I am drawn to a quote that I read a year ago by A. W. Tozer, who said, "It is doubtful whether God can bless a man greatly until He has hurt him deeply."

> "It is doubtful whether God can bless a man greatly until He has hurt him deeply." –A.W. Tozer

While it is true that as children, things happen to us that we cannot always control, as adults, we do have the ability to make choices. We can seek help. We can choose life and have the faith that facing our problems may help others find solutions to their problems. We also have choices in the way we respond to bullying.

If you have been bullied or are being bullied, get help. Talk to your parents, a friend, or a relative. Talk to a professional therapist or counselor, if possible. You may be tough and endure, but the invisible scars won't heal properly unless you rip off the dirty Band-Aids and allow cleansing and the application of healing medicine.

Not all experts agree that bullying leads to teen suicide. But as a victim of bullying, I agree with the Centers for Disease Control and Prevention research that shows that bullying behavior and suicide-related behavior are linked.[14]

Maybe I took too many symbolic logic classes (if *A* implies *B*, and *B* implies *C*, then *A* implies *C*), but if teen suicide is often a result of depression, and bullying can cause depression, then *bullying needs to stop.*

If you are reading this book and have struggled with depression, talk to a professional who can help you. Do not wait. Do not tell yourself that you'll feel better. Parents, don't let your children fool you. If they are acting differently than usual, be a parent and talk to them or encourage them to talk to a professional. Do it *now*, not when it's convenient.

Many parents have access to a twenty-four/seven nurse line or EAP line through their health-insurance plans that can help even after business hours or on weekends. There are also hotlines for people who are suicidal.

Don't self-medicate when it comes to depression. My mother was bipolar (known as manic-depression back in the day). Twice, I found her after she had tried to commit suicide. I was told that there had been previous attempts when I was too young to realize what was happening.

My great sadness is that when she was struggling with mental illness, the options were very limited and not always helpful. Today we know so much more about the chemical imbalances that can lead to depression or mania; however, you (unless you are a licensed professional) and I are not medical experts and need to seek help in these situations.

Lesson learned: Seeking help is really the brave thing to do!

Questions for Reflection

1. What resources do you think could help you heal emotionally?
2. Why is it important to use the resources available to you?
3. What obstacles exist that might make it difficult for you to access resources?
4. How can you overcome these obstacles?
5. List one goal you have for yourself in talking to a professional.

PART III
Join the Revolution

9

"Crazy"

Home Sweet Home

My alcoholic father divorced my mentally ill mother after thirty years of marriage. I was thirteen when they decided to divorce, and that was a dark time in my life. I was being bullied at school, I was not happy with my physical appearance, and now I was going to be minus one parent. Well, not for long.

My father remarried when I was sixteen. I was relieved for many reasons, but my relief soon turned to angst (once again, that's a topic for another book). While my father was dating the person who would become my stepmother, she couldn't have endeared herself more to me and to my younger sister. She even made a positive impression on my eighteen-year-old brother, who was halfway across the country attending college.

I started to believe that maybe I could have a couple of normal high-school years. I'd lost a bunch of weight by that time, and now there was someone new in my life who wasn't mentally ill and would treat me like a daughter. Never mind that she already had two daughters and a son (who happened to be my age). I knew that my sister and I would be treated well, and I was so looking forward to that.

A switch flipped. They were married, and the games began. Soon after their nuptials, my new stepmother rejoiced in telling me that I was a terrible housekeeper. Okay, I thought, I've only been doing it for about seven years. (My mom had been mostly manic or depressive during the seven years leading up to the divorce—she was seldom in a stable state of mind.) I accepted her criticism at first, and then I shot back. "I'm a kid," I told her. "I'm not supposed to be a good housekeeper."

She replied, "Your father has bragged about what a wonderful job you've done cooking and cleaning, but I don't think you're much of a housekeeper."

Can you imagine a woman in her forties telling her brand-new stepdaughter this? Seriously? I thought. Are you kidding me?

Since I was nine years old, my brother, who was two years older, and I had been doing more and more of the cooking, most of the cleaning, the grocery shopping, the laundry, the bill paying, and looking after our sister. I was naïve enough to believe that I wouldn't find bullies in my home and that at least I would have one safe haven. I was wrong.

I realized the sad truth very quickly. This woman had serious (probably undiagnosed) issues not unlike those of my poor mom. My father had traded for more of the same.

My First Job

I decided that since I was going to college, I needed to get a job. I hadn't been able to work outside the home previously because I'd had too many responsibilities. But now I could! I talked to my father and stepmother about getting a job, and my father was supportive, as long as my grades didn't slip. I wasn't the straight-A student that the brother two years my senior was, but I was in the top 10 percent of my class and didn't believe my grades would suffer.

I wanted to work at Stouffer's restaurant, located at the big regional mall nearby. My stepmother drove me to the interview and agreed that it would be a decent job for me, although she couldn't resist bursting my bubble by telling me that I probably wouldn't be hired because I had no experience as a server. Again, I had to love her positive attitude. Well, the manager did offer me the job. I remember hanging up the phone after I got the call and eagerly telling my stepmother the good news.

"How do you plan to get to work?" she asked.

I told her that I assumed she would let me borrow her car, since she didn't work, and the car sat idle all-day long. But I should have realized that her answer would be no, as I wasn't even allowed to drive to school. Nope, it was great fun being the only senior on my bus.

Anyway, I tried to engage my father to convince my stepmother to let me drive her car, but he couldn't be bothered. There were streetcars that ran though the suburbs of Pittsburgh, but I would have had a hike on a very busy road from the streetcar stop to my job. So, I had to call the restaurant manager back and turn down the job. I had no reliable way of getting to work and no support from my parental units.

I was pretty upset about turning down my first job offer, but I eventually got a job within walking distance. Again, my stepmother couldn't resist destroying my enthusiasm. She told me that she didn't know why I felt I needed to work at a minimum-wage job and that I should begin thinking about a career. I told her that I was going to college to prepare for a career. She replied that she did not think I needed to go to college and that she would make sure I didn't get a penny of help from my father.

Finally, I couldn't take any more of her crap. I asked her why she resented me so much and why she had a problem with my going to college. She said neither of her daughters went to college, and the only viable reason for "someone like me" going to college was to find a man.

"Someone like me?" I puzzled.

I was never more motivated to go to college. I applied to any college that would accept me—as long as it was miles away. I even solicited information from colleges in California and Hawaii because I couldn't get far enough away from that crazy, bitter woman.

Senior Prom

When it came time for my senior prom, my stepmother insisted that I take her son (my stepbrother). We didn't go to the same high school, so she didn't see a problem with that. I did. I refused, and when one of my classmates asked me to the prom, I flatly told him no. I wasn't going to the prom. I tried to make a silly joke out of it, because I was too humiliated to tell him the truth: if I went to the prom, it would be with my stepbrother, because my stepmother said so.

I had lived through a great deal of humiliation by then, and there was no way I was going to add to it by taking my stepbrother to my high-school prom. That would have been the finishing touch to four years that I desperately wanted to escape.

What has nagged at me for years is the fact that the guy who did ask me to the prom committed suicide shortly after graduation. We never dated. In fact, I was kind of shocked when he asked me to go to prom with him. We were both in the band, but I was still the old "fat and ugly Mary," according to my own self-perception. Who in the world would ask me to the prom? Maybe someone who had his own demons. While I don't think I had anything to do with his suicide, it has haunted me for years.

Was he struggling? Did he need a friend? Did he need someone to talk to? I heard after his death that he had applied to a military academy and wasn't accepted. I'll never know what was going on in his head, because while it was probably understandable, I was too self-absorbed in my own pain to think about someone else.

> ...I was too self-absorbed in my own pain to think about someone else.

And so, It Goes...

I really didn't have much contact with my stepmother after college. She made it a point to tell me that I was not welcome back home after I graduated. I felt like the opposite of Dorothy in *The Wizard of Oz*. There was no place like home, all right. And I didn't exactly have a yellow brick road to follow, so I did exactly what she said I would do. I met a guy at college, got married, and then divorced four years later.

However, I also got a degree and started a career. I eventually met a great guy and have been married to him for almost thirty years. We didn't go "home" to visit often; it was just too depressing to be around my father and my stepmother.

My father died on Thanksgiving Day 1990. I got a call from my stepmother at about 7:30 a.m. I had done a great deal of baking the night before, as we had planned to spend the day with my husband's family. When my husband awoke, I told him that my father had passed away that morning and that I needed to go to Pittsburgh to help my stepmother with arrangements.

Did I want to go? Heck, no. I was sad because there were things I would have liked to have told my father before he died. But why would I want to help a woman who had shown nothing but contempt for me since the day she married my father? But I was the only one among my siblings who was available to help her, so off I went.

When I arrived at her house (the house I grew up in—the only home I'd lived in until I moved away), I had a knot in my stomach. I didn't have a lot of happy memories in that house, and I figured that the next few days would add to that list.

I knocked on the door, and my stepmother greeted me as though she were happy to see me. I think she was just happy to see anybody so she wouldn't have to work out the details alone. Her two daughters were already at the house. We quickly said our hellos and got down to business. It had been decided that I would accompany my stepmother to the funeral home to help her pick out a container for my father's ashes. He wanted to be cremated and had stated in his will that he wanted his ashes spread out West over the mountains in Arizona.

I was grateful that my stepmother chose one of the better local funeral homes to help with the arrangements. The funeral director and I had known each other for years. There weren't many options for containers for ashes, though. They all looked like glorified milk cartons to me, and choosing one of the two or three options seemed kind of ridiculous. Certainly, my stepmother could have made the selection.

Once we picked out his "final resting container," my stepmother announced that I needed to say good-bye to my father.

What the heck? Is he still alive? I wondered. "What do you mean?" I asked.

"I think you need closure, and you need to say good-bye to your father. Follow me." I obediently got up and followed her and the funeral director to an institutional-looking room, where, I surmised, they prepared the bodies. My father's body was on a gurney of sorts. My stepmother went over, kissed the corpse on the forehead, and demanded that I do the same.

"Nope," I replied. I turned around and walked out of the funeral home.

When we got home, my stepmother informed me that she had already found a life-insurance policy of my father's that she'd known nothing about and that I was the sole beneficiary. Mind you, he had just died a few hours earlier. Turned out that he had a larger policy of which she was the beneficiary and the ten-thousand-dollar policy that he had never mentioned to her—or to me, for that matter. She made it quite clear that she was furious about that second policy and that she was planning to contact her attorney to contest it. I told her that I really didn't want the money anyway. I couldn't have cared less.

She was very unhappy when she learned a few days later that she could not contest his naming of me as the beneficiary of the small policy. She also made sure to tell me that my father had very specific instructions as to how the money was to be divided among my siblings. I thanked her for letting me know and told her that I would divide the money equally, which I did.

I was determined that I was done letting her push me around and control me. We didn't have much to say to each other after that. Thankfully, she went to bed early, so I didn't have to make polite conversation with her. After the memorial service, a few days later, we said our good-byes. I thought I'd have very little interaction, if any, with her from that point on.

That Aching Back

Two months later, my husband had surgery to remove a herniated disk in his back. A week after his surgery, my stepmother called and asked if I wanted the bedroom set that had been mine as a young girl.

"Yes," I responded. "Thank you so much for asking. I have a little niece who would love that furniture." This bedroom set was quite old, but it was white with gold trim, and my niece dreamed of having a white bedroom set. This would be a wonderful surprise for her.

Then the other shoe dropped. My stepmother informed me that I would have to pick it up within two days.

I explained that my husband had just had back surgery and was on crutches, an ice storm was headed our way, and there was no way I could leave him alone or find help on such short notice, let alone get there safely!

That was irrelevant to her. "That's your problem," she said. "I'm having new carpeting put in upstairs, and I want that furniture out of there."

Once again, I tried my best powers of persuasion and used my negotiating skills, but it was to no avail. "Look," I said. "I'm sure you know I would be there this weekend if I could, but I simply can't. My husband needs me here for a few more days, and I'm nervous about driving a U-Haul truck by myself in adverse weather. Can you please just have your son-in-law put the furniture in the basement or the garage until I can get it out?" That seemed like a reasonable request to me. I even offered to drive out in my own car to help move the furniture.

She informed me that the furniture would be on the sidewalk come Monday morning. If I wanted it badly enough, I'd find a way to pick it up. Otherwise, the trash men or someone else scouring the street for bargains would get it.

I told her then that I thought she was the meanest, nastiest person I'd ever met in my life and that I desired no further contact with her. I hung up the phone in tears. I couldn't believe she was taking my stuff and discarding it just because she could. I had two brothers who were close enough in proximity to help, and when they realized what she'd done, they wondered why I didn't ask them to pick up the furniture. I told them that I thought this woman was borderline evil, and I'd just as soon not subject anyone in the family to her dysfunction any more than necessary. Besides, I'm a hopeless optimist; I think good wins out over evil in the long run.

Lesson learned: Find your own yellow brick road, and follow it!

Questions for Reflection

1. Have you known anyone who was bullied by a family member?
2. What options exist for someone in this situation?

3. What's the difference between a parent or an adult being strict versus being a bully?

4. How can you help someone who has been belittled or bullied by a family member?

5. How can blended family members overcome the temptation to put each other down?

10

"Twist and Shout"

You Are Not the Boss of Me

I realize that work is work, but we can take a cue from generation Y. We spend 30–40 percent of our time at work, so unless your job is a professional acting gig, it's important to be able to be your authentic self at work. To do this, you must fit in with the culture. If you don't, what are you doing there?

Like most working adults, I've left a few companies over the years. Some resignations were mixed with doubt and second thoughts, while others were a race to exit as quickly as possible. During my years as a human-resource professional, I always joked that I became friends with some of my associates only after leaving an organization. It was hard for me to become friends with my coworkers when I had to balance the needs of the organization and the needs of the associates day after day.

At one point, I had left a company with no anxiety or second thoughts. It was definitely time to go. I remember getting a call shortly afterward from one of my former coworkers. He wanted to meet for coffee. He wanted to understand why I'd left. Didn't I like my job?

By the time we met, I had already begun a new job and was fully immersed in my new role. Still, the questions continued. I explained that I had worked for someone who was extraordinarily bright and could turn on the charisma as if it were a lamp; however, this individual wasn't a good leader. In fact, this person was extremely manipulative and autocratic. One of the components of this company's corporate culture was that people could supposedly be their authentic selves at work. But this positional leader didn't know how to coach and didn't know how to make genuine connections with others. This boss expected everyone to be just like him.

No matter where I was, I was determined to be authentically me.

I think it bothered this boss that I was a night owl. I would arrive no later than 9:00 a.m. every day, and I would work until 7:30 p.m. or 8:00 p.m. most days and take work home most evenings and weekends. I got the feeling that my boss wanted to be the last to leave, and consequently, he resented the fact that I not only worked later than he did but that I also worked on weekends. I was a self-admitted workaholic, but there was also too much work assigned to my team. Nothing we did was automated. We shuffled stacks of paper, which was nuts, considering the efficiencies that existed for the type of work we did. There was always just too much that needed to be done.

I also needed to lose some weight, and my boss had told me after a wellness meeting a few months earlier that I needed to set an example. Geez, I thought. I don't smoke, I don't really drink, and my biometric screenings were very good, except for needing to lose weight. However, the longer I worked for this individual, the higher my blood pressure rose. That was the reason I decided to leave when I did. I knew that my boss did not appreciate that I was not a cookie-cutter, carbon copy of him; he'd made that clear to me in one of our final conversations.

I was certainly not drinking his Kool-Aid every morning—I preferred my coffee.

I needed to work where I could be my authentic self. I also couldn't work for someone who bullied others and then denied that those conversations took place.

We all should show respect to our superiors at work. If you feel as though you can't, then it's time to leave. If you are in school, however, you may have to endure. You don't have to suffer bullying, but you may have to put up with a member of the faculty who wants to put you in a box. Realize that this is a short-term problem. It may seem like an eternity while you are in high school, but it will pass more quickly than you think.

Like employers, there are many wonderful educators, and there are some who would be fired if not for tenure. Life isn't fair. There's no point in getting upset about it. You are in charge of you (unless you are a minor, in which case your parents or legal guardians have a say).

Did I Ask for Your Opinion?

Several months ago, my doorbell rang. A young man in a T-shirt and jeans stood on my front porch. I noticed a red pickup truck in the driveway with two other young men sitting in it. I didn't open my storm door; I talked through it, as I had no idea who this kid was or what he wanted. He told me he was going door to door and wanted to know if I wanted an estimate on getting our driveway sealed. I explained that the driveway had been put in just eighteen months ago, and it was suggested that we not seal the driveway for at least three to five years.

The kid looked at me like I was completely stupid. "Who told you that?" he asked.

"The person who put the driveway in," I replied.

He shook his head and stated, "Your driveway needs to be sealed now."

"Well, I beg to differ with you," I said. "And further, when it does need to be sealed, my husband and I plan to do it ourselves."

Now, this kid had never met my husband and had no idea who I was. I just happened to be at home answering the door when he showed up. His response was priceless.

"Well," he said, "if you two do it, it's gonna look like a piece of shit."

"Well, thanks so much for the positive encouragement!" I said as he walked dejectedly back to the truck.

Where had he learned this behavior? I wondered. At home? Did his parents call everyone who didn't agree with them an idiot? I realize that he needed to earn a living, but there's an old saying: "You catch more flies with honey than with vinegar." I will remember this young man; there is *no way* he or his friends will ever be invited to do any work at my house. Would you believe that he had the nerve to come back a week later and corner my husband, who happened to be home?

Fortunately, I had already told him about this kid; he kind of chuckled, thanked the young man, and told him we had it covered.

It really bugs me when people you don't know and from whom you didn't ask for help suddenly call you a jerk because you didn't buy their product or service. Really? And here's the irony of that situation. I did contact the man who had installed our asphalt driveway. He came out, examined it, and begged me not to ruin his work by putting sealer on it.

Huh? I thought.

He told me that there were no signs of deterioration and that over time, sealing can do more harm than good. I won't go into the entire explanation, but this guy has been pouring driveways for many, many years, so we trusted him. I assured him that we would contact him before even considering sealing it in the future!

Choose Your Words

Parents need to take a serious look at the adage that most people learn in kindergarten (except

...choose your words carefully.

me, because I didn't go to kindergarten); choose your words carefully. Truly be intentional about what comes out of your mouth when someone disagrees with you. Do you love your enemies, or do you spew venomous diatribes? And worse, do you do this in front of your kids?

One of the most popular shows on TV when I was a child was *All in the Family,* starring Jean Stapleton as Edith Bunker and Carroll O'Connor as Archie Bunker, a bigoted, racist bully. Their daughter, Gloria, was played by Sally Struthers, and in hindsight, she was either a remarkable character or the writers really blew it. How could she possibly have turned out to be so kind and caring (like her TV mom) when her TV dad was the biggest jerk you could imagine?

A few months ago, I received a phone call from an older gentleman calling on behalf of a nonprofit organization. He stated that he just needed a moment of my time and wasn't trying to sell me anything or ask for money. He proceeded to tell me about the excellent work his organization had been doing to help save the lives of children and asked if I would be kind enough to commit to mailing literature to my neighbors. I did this once before for another nonprofit and knew that I did not have the time to volunteer. As politely as I could, I explained that my husband and I had a full summer (which we did) and that I really couldn't commit to that project.

He replied that it would only take ten minutes. I knew that it would take longer. I repeated that I could not help him, but I was certain he would find someone in our area who would be happy to do it.

He then became agitated and inquired if I would instead make a donation.

Hmm. "Gosh," I said. "I thought you told me you weren't asking for money. Sir, I appreciate that you have some goals to accomplish today, and so do I. I regret that I am unable to help you and hope that you have a wonderful day."

Sadly, the nonprofit organization he represents will suffer. Who would support it when it has people with bad attitudes calling prospective donors on its behalf? Yes, it is a worthwhile organization, but it decided to allow this person to represent it. This man was snippy with me and crossed the line. He became unprofessional because my answer wasn't a resounding yes. While this might not rise to the level of bullying, it was annoying. He employed guilt tactics, and I resented his persistence. I shouldn't have been made to feel bad because I had priorities that didn't align with his. I also didn't want to hang up on him and be as rude as he was to me.

Nonprofit organizations would be wise to choose their telephone solicitors carefully. I can't tell you how many bullies have called my home representing well-known organizations. Maybe that tactic works for some, but it sure doesn't work for me.

Lesson learned: If you can't say anything nice, don't say anything at all.

Questions for Reflection

1. Have you ever worked for a bully-boss or known someone who has? How did this affect you or them?
2. Why is it important to stand up to bully-bosses? What's the likely outcome if you don't?
3. Have you ever been bullied by a solicitor (in person or on the phone)? How did it make you feel? What did you do?
4. How will you respond to rude or bullying solicitors in the future?
5. Why is it important for you not to bully solicitors or others who call you unexpectedly?

11

"Doctor, Doctor"

Young Doctor—the "I'm Smarter Than You Are" Bully

In April 2009, I decided to make an appointment with a dermatologist for a baseline assessment. I was over fifty, and having been a fair-haired and blue-eyed child who had experienced more than a couple of sunburns, I thought it was important. Both of my parents had been diagnosed with skin cancer. In addition, I had this "thing" on my back that was annoying. It was some sort of growth in the middle of my back, and it was really itchy.

I made an appointment with a female dermatologist at a local practice just minutes from my house. I didn't have a referral from anyone, but her practice was in my health-insurance network. How many times have we made medical decisions because a doctor was or wasn't in our health-insurance network?

I walked in for the appointment, completed the obligatory paper work, and was eventually summoned to the examining room. I was asked to disrobe except for my underwear. Yep, I could retain a smidgeon of dignity by keeping my underwear intact.

You can imagine my surprise when a young male doctor walked into my examining room. I had requested a woman, so what the heck? It was hard enough for me to stand practically naked in an examining room with my obviously middle-aged physique—but to be examined by someone young enough to be my son? Well, that made a huge dent in my already-fragile ego. Initially, the young doctor was very nice, sensing my obvious insecurity. He explained that the doctors in the practice rotate, and when a patient makes an appointment, he or she could be seen by anyone in the practice. Lucky me!

He examined every part of my body, which I knew needed to be done. That's why I was there. I mentioned the growth in the middle of my back that hadn't been there very long and was quite itchy. My husband had developed the habit of not scratching the middle of my back, which was precisely where it itched. I relayed this to the dermatologist. He looked at it and told me it didn't look like anything. He said not to worry about it.

Again, I explained that its location, under my bra, was kind of annoying. Again, he told me that in his (expert) opinion, I should ignore it. It was probably an age-related growth.

Okay. I knew I was no spring chicken, but I didn't need to be reminded that around the magical age of fifty, your skin really changes. You could have played a lengthy game of connect the dots on my skin. Still, I wanted this thing off my back. I finally said, "Can't you just lance it? I have three family members who are doctors, and they've all had moles lanced."

The doctor stated, "This is not a mole, and if I lance it, you will have to pay the lab fee."

"Really?" I said. "Please take it off. It's itchy, and it bothers me." That was my third reference to itchiness—you try hooking a bra over that and tell me how comfortable you are all day.

The doctor finally grabbed a blade and grudgingly scraped it off my back. After applying the standard Band-Aid, he assured me that he was 99 percent certain that the growth was nothing more than an age-related keratosis and that I would hear back from him in five to seven days.

Otherwise, I passed the examination with flying colors. You can imagine my surprise just three days later when I received a phone call from the doctor while I was at work. He began the conversation by asking me if I was sitting down. I told him that I was at work, at my desk, and yes, I was sitting down.

He then stated that the lab results had come back and that I had melanoma. I almost dropped the phone. He was already moving into my next steps when I rudely interrupted him.

"Wait just a minute," I said. "You mean to tell me I have melanoma, the skin cancer that if left unchecked would metastasize in various organs and eventually kill me? The skin cancer that would likely have taken my life in the next three to five years had I not been diagnosed?"

"Well, I prefer not to think of it that way," he said.

"What?" I replied. "That's the only way I *can* think about it. If I had not insisted that you lance that growth on my back, I would be dead in the next three to five years."

"Probably," he said.

I felt that this doctor had subtly tried to bully me during the examination. He had refused to remove the mole because it didn't look like a mole to him. He had tried to intimidate me and honestly made me feel like a hypochondriac. This was a very innocuous type of bullying, much like the method used by the narcissistic boss, but it was bullying all the same. I thanked him for calling me and told him I would take it from there. I told him that I would no longer be under his care and that I would find a competent dermatologist who listened to his patients.

What was most troubling to me when I moved into research mode was that this growth was irregular in shape, had grown quickly, and it itched. All were possible signs of melanoma, according to my own online inquiries.

Scarred for Life

I knew I was going to be in good hands at our renowned local cancer hospital, which is where I'd been scheduled to meet with an oncologist. This hospital had been my client in a former career, and I loved it. But I didn't know anything about skin cancer. In fact, I used to think skin cancer was no big deal. That ignorance was trumped once I began to really educate myself about basal cell, squamous cell, and melanoma skin cancers.

I was blessed with a wonderful oncologist and surgeon. He was kind, compassionate, and knew that I was scared to death. He didn't sugarcoat anything, but I knew that I was in good hands. The staff members were just as I'd hoped they would be. They were competent, caring, and encouraging. My surgeon removed all the cancer (I was at stage 2). Thankfully, I did not need radiation or chemotherapy. I was never going to be invited to pursue a career as a model, and I was thankful that wasn't how I earned my living.

To this day, I have a deep divot in the middle of my back. But that scar is a daily joyful reminder that I stood up for myself when a young, arrogant doctor just out of medical school tried to intimidate me with his intelligence. I realize every day that had I not advocated for myself and demanded that he remove the growth, I would most likely not be alive to type these pages. In this instance, standing up to bullying and intimidation literally saved my life.

Lesson learned: Advocate for yourself! Don't let professionals dismiss your concerns or back you into a corner!

Questions for Reflection

1. Has a professional ever used bully behavior on you? What did he or she do? How did it make you feel?
2. What resources do you have (friends, family, church) to talk to?
3. What action can you take in the future?
4. What could prevent you from taking that action?
5. How can you overcome those challenges?

12

"Take This Job and Shove It!"

As I look back at school, I realize that bullies don't have boundaries. They have the potential to bully anywhere, in any setting, and in any situation. It's important to stand up to bullies, regardless of where they appear.

I encountered my first professional bully very early in my career. I went to work for a manufacturing company after graduating from college. This was quite interesting because the Equal Employment Opportunity Commission (EEOC) was charged with writing the first guidelines on sexual harassment that year. Unfortunately, I doubt that the workers at that plant were familiar with the EEOC's work. (Isn't it interesting that in 1980 we finally realized that sexual harassment was occurring and should be illegal; and here we are almost forty years later, and bullying is neither diminishing, nor is it illegal.)

My First Workplace Bully

My first job was that of manager trainee. I was supposed to be trained over a period of twelve to eighteen months to become a supervisor in a manufacturing plant in Pennsylvania. I was elated, as I was one of only two women chosen for this newly created program.

Management trainees were expected to work/train in all areas of the manufacturing plant. I actually enjoyed most of my experiences there, despite the catcalls and whistles every time I entered the plant. Really? Me? Let me introduce myself. They used to call me fat and ugly in high school…and oddly enough, that's how I still felt inside. So, while their harassment was inappropriate, it was also oddly surprising to me.

Usually, the workers stopped with the whistles and such once they got to know me. I could talk football and guns with them, so I was able to fit in and, therefore, avoid being singled out because of my gender—that is, until I entered the machine shop. The machine-shop supervisor was expected to train me on key processes in this area of the plant. This guy made Archie Bunker, the TV character I mentioned earlier, look like a peach. He truly became my worst nightmare.

This supervisor ignored me for the entire eight weeks that I was in his department. I observed him watching me a few times and sneering at me as he talked to some of the other workers. I learned what I could by watching others and jumping in when I wasn't putting myself at risk of losing a finger or an arm. And that fear was very real to me. During my training experience, a coil of steel that was not properly secured crushed an employee to death. In addition, I noticed more than a couple of workers in this department who lacked a digit or two. I was willing to work hard, but I wasn't willing to risk losing a finger or my life just to fit in.

When it came time for my review, the machine-shop supervisor slammed me. He gave me a poor rating overall. It didn't matter to him that every other department I'd trained in for the past year had given me an excellent rating. He was so cruel that I found myself tearing up in our review meeting. The more I tried to fight it, the more easily the tears flowed down my cheeks. I refused to sign the review and proceeded directly to the human-resource (HR) department, where I talked to the director of HR.

The HR director was a very kind man. He had hired me. He was very disturbed by this supervisor's treatment of me and concurred that everyone else thought I was doing well in the program and that I was well liked. In fact, the head of a department in which I'd already trained had expressed interest in hiring me to work full time.

However, at the tender age of twenty-two, I wanted to send a message. I didn't have another job to run to, but I was determined that enough was enough. This may have been the first time I'd left a job without having another, but it would not be the last. I wanted the director of HR and others to know that I did not want to work in a company that allowed leaders like the machine-shop supervisor to get away with this type of treatment.

I must have been incredibly naïve. I thought the machine-shop supervisor should have been given a below-standard review for not doing *his* job and for not helping me during those eight weeks. From my perspective, the fact that he wasn't going to lose his job or even be reprimanded was unthinkable. I walked into the HR office within a week of our last meeting and resigned. This sent a mild wave of concern throughout the company because I was one of only a few women hired in the program. And the fact was I had done an excellent job in all assignments other than the machine shop.

I soon found an "interim" job that lasted almost fourteen years! I realized that while it might have been wiser for me to have landed a new job before resigning, I was determined not to put up with a bully again. Having endured four years of bullying in high school and several years of being bullied in grade school and middle school, enough was enough. I was finding my voice.

Other Workplace Bullies

Sadly, I've endured additional workplace bullies who also exhibited racism, religious hypocrisy, and narcissism. I had one supervisor who demanded that I serve beverages during an important meeting even though I was the highest-ranking executive he had at the time. He reasoned that his guests, who all happened to be male, would be more comfortable if a woman served drinks than if a man did.

I ended up leaving organizations because of bully-bosses. Some were my supervisors; some weren't. But the fact is, they all made life miserable for those who worked closely with them. And they all took advantage of their positions of power in their respective organizations. They led by command and control, and if you didn't follow them, you were doomed.

Workplace bullies are abusive, intimidating, sabotaging, threatening, and humiliating. This isn't something we should tolerate or accept. Becoming a certified leadership trainer, speaker, and coach has reinforced my belief that effective leaders lead through positive influence, not through position power—and certainly not through intimidation.

> **Workplace bullies are abusive, intimidating, sabotaging, threatening, and humiliating.**

Because of my experience with bullies, I was bound and determined that I wasn't going to let anyone have that type of control over me again. I've left more than one company largely because of a workplace bully who was not held accountable, even when I wasn't always the target. However, in each situation, a company leader was not being held accountable, and I refused to stand by and ignore what was happening. Fortunately, in each instance, I was able to land a new position a brief time later. I've never been independently wealthy, and every time I left a position without having another job lined up, I was taking a huge risk. But I've long believed Mel Thompson, who said, "If you don't stand for something, you stand for nothing." These were risks I was willing to take to live by my principles.

I believe that each of these bully-bosses will be judged someday, just as I will. But I know that in each situation, I brought attention to their bullying so that others might not have to endure their inappropriate antics in the future. Workplace bullies are truly reprehensible, and unfortunately, there seems to be no shortage of them.

I once received a somewhat desperate e-mail from a woman I had worked with. She asked if we could meet. During our conversation, she explained that she had recently been placed on medication for depression. What? I'd known this person for several years, and she never seemed to be anything other than happy and content. She was known to get a little stressed every now and then, just like many of us, but depression was serious. I didn't see that coming at all.

I asked my friend what she thought was causing her depression. In a word, she said, "Work." "It's my job. I hate it. And I hate my new department head."

Funny, I thought. I remember a new boss who made my life miserable too. I asked her specifically what was going on. She gave me a few examples that involved her department head ignoring her and withholding information from her. This individual also gave others feedback about my friend that was never delivered in person. The worst of it was that she had been asked to develop competencies in areas in which she wasn't skilled. In other words, she had to go to work every day and fake being someone else. Why? Because a bully department head told someone else to tell her that she did!

A fellow author recently shared the following anonymous quote that she'd found in her Franklin Planner. "The definition of hell is living someone else's life."

The Revolution

I am fighting a war, and it's not overseas. The battles are right here in our communities, our churches, our schools, our businesses, and even in the political arena. Like most wars, this one has produced far too many casualties and has gone on far too long. It's time to take a stand against bullying and the damaging psychological imprint it leaves on people. When will arrogant, egotistical bully-leaders learn that we all have unique sets of talents and gifts? Some of us will never be very good at certain things, and that's okay. Great leaders tap into people's strengths and build effective teams based on talent, not on blind spots or weaknesses. Stephen Covey got it right when he said, "The role of the leader is to foster mutual respect and build a complementary team where each strength is made productive and each weakness irrelevant."

I'm proud that I encouraged my friend to quit her job because she was being bullied, and I'm relieved that she eventually did. She was worried because, like me, she was not independently wealthy and needed to work. And, like me, she loves to work—if the job is in her strength zone. On the day that she handed in her resignation, she was offered another job through a friend of a friend. Coincidental? I think you get back what you give out. She is a great person and a hard worker. She gives far more than she receives. She got back what she gave out.

If you're a bully, you're going to attract other toxic bullies. Dedicated, motivated, authentic people probably won't be drawn to you. The sad fact is that it only takes one bully in leadership to poison a company by creating a cancerous corporate culture.

On the other hand, if you're a good person and respectful of others, you'll find that other great people are drawn to you like a magnet. And if you stay true to yourself, as my friend did, you will get exactly what you need and what you deserve!

Garbage In/Garbage Out

So, the world isn't fair, and bad things do happen to good people. Most of us have and will face bullies in our lifetimes. Whether the bullying is delivered in person, in writing, or in cyberspace, you are in charge of you! How you respond to the insults and what you allow into your head will dramatically affect you for perhaps the rest of your life!

I didn't realize until rather late in life that our subconscious mind is like the biggest storage system you can imagine. When we allow negative thoughts into our minds, it isn't always easy to get them out. Negative thoughts are like cockroaches or bedbugs, and it takes a major extermination effort to eradicate them.

You can't just introduce positive thoughts occasionally. You really must choose to let go of what we refer to in the coaching industry as *limiting beliefs*. Here are a few practical guidelines for dealing with the garbage that bullies try to fling at us:

1. **Time out**. When someone insults you or bullies you, allow yourself to become angry or mad (for a moment). This should help you to avoid internalizing the anger. Don't react or respond immediately; just give yourself the freedom to be upset. Don't act out toward the other person. Go take a walk or walk away. But allow yourself to feel angry and not worthless.

2. **Boundaries**. Recognize that you need to establish healthy boundaries. That means you shouldn't hang around with "mean girls" or the people who bully you.

3. **Support group**. Make sure you surround yourself with family and/or friends who build you up. I used to work for a company that employed a lot of minimum-wage employees. I would coach the managers of those workers to understand that for many of those employees, coming to work might just be the best part of their day.

4. **Tell someone**. If someone has physically harmed you, report it. If you are a minor, tell your parents or your guardian. If they do nothing, tell the police. If you are not a minor, tell the police. Think about this. If someone has physically harmed you, he or she is likely to hurt someone else. And, who knows if he or she will become more aggressive toward you? If any type of assault happens at school, report it to the principal, as well. I've run across at least one bully who fit the description of a sociopath. Sociopaths have no conscience, and they are manipulative. They need serious help from mental-health professionals. You cannot and should not stand up to them alone!

5. **Suicide hotline**. If you feel suicidal or have had suicidal thoughts, call the National Suicide Hotline at 1-800-273-8255. It is staffed by trained professionals who can and do want to help you.

6. **Have fun**. Make sure you take time to focus on a hobby or outlet that you really enjoy. Maybe it's playing sports, a musical instrument, doing crafts, drawing, painting, working with animals, or visiting the elderly. Do something positive or constructive that makes you feel good!

7. **Confront or quit**. If you work for a bully-boss, try to find someone in your company whom you can trust and confide in. Maybe your bully-boss isn't aware of how he or she is coming across, and you could approach him or her. If it's completely intolerable, the boss is unapproachable, and you can't afford to quit, consider the impact of a temporary loss of income versus the damage that is being inflicted on your psyche. If you are like me, you'll quit anyway and trust that things will work out. But you must make choices that you can live with.

    The reality is that many bully-bosses get impressive results. Too many weak corporate leaders confuse getting results with effective leadership. Adolf Hitler got results (for a while) but at what cost? I know that's an extreme example. The point is, business owners should show more concern for their employees' well-being rather than lining their pockets with gold generated by a bully-leader.

8. **Forgive**. Learn to forgive. Most bullies are probably not sociopaths. They may have been bullied themselves. The best medicine for you, the victim, is to forgive your bully. Forgiveness is tough for some, and it's been difficult for me. However, when you harbor ill feelings toward someone, he or she generally is not aware of it, and the bitterness that you hold on to can prevent you from experiencing true joy and happiness.

9. **Exercise**. Sometimes just going for a walk can change a mood from sullen and depressed to energetic and hopeful. If you don't feel like going outside, you can march in place and do stretching exercises. Really, there's no excuse. Do something to get your endorphins working. Endorphins are the chemicals released when we exercise, meditate, laugh, etc. Generally, they make us feel better and reduce stress.

10. **Pray**. Pray and/or meditate. For many of us, this is the best place to start.

Final Thanks

I am grateful for those superiors to whom I reported who were not bully-bosses and didn't allow bullying to exist in the workplace. I've recognized *some* of them in my acknowledgments. I am indebted to those supervisors who respect the uniqueness and authenticity that we each have as human beings for their approach to leadership, which, sadly, is still a bit rare.

To those of you in leadership positions who turn a blind eye to bullying (whether in school, church, the workplace, or government), I hope that you carefully consider the psychological and physiological damage you are inflicting on those in your charge. Bullying sucks. It's not healthy. It's not required in the workplace, and it's not appropriate anywhere in a civilized society. And just like sexual harassment, it doesn't *belong* in the workplace. And I'm just optimistic enough to believe that with the right leadership in government and business, it will be illegal someday.

Lesson learned: Stand for something, and lead from wherever you can!

Questions for reflection

1. What responsibility do we have to speak up for coworkers or others who have been bullied?

2. What causes us to be silent bystanders?

3. What would you do if someone confided in you that he or she had been bullied?

4. What would you do if he or she asked you to keep this information in confidence?

5. What would you do if someone confessed to you that he or she had bullied someone else?

APPENDIX A

Action Plan

Because of reading *Right of Passage*, the most important action I can take to help myself or someone else is to _____
_____
_____

As a result, I will…
Start doing
a.
b.
c.

Stop doing
a.
b.
c.

Continue doing
a.
b.
c.

I will ask _____ to be my accountability partner to ensure I complete my action plan!

APPENDIX B

Bullying Myth Busters

Myth	Reality
1. Bullying is a rite of passage.	1. We've accepted this as an excuse to condone childhood bullying. But childhood bullying is not normal, and bullies have since left the playground and are in leadership positions.
2. Only unpopular people get bullied.	2. Not true. A 2014 study titled *Popular Kids Face Greater Risk of Getting Bullied*[15] paints a very different picture. And even if it were true, why is that acceptable?
3. Only kids who have been bullied bully others.	3. Some, but not all bullies are actually victims of bullying.

Myth	Reality
4. Sticks and stones will break your bones, but names will never hurt you.	4. Words do hurt and can remain imprinted in our subconscious minds for eternity, if we don't know how to clean them out!
5. People are too sensitive. No one can really make you feel bad about yourself. You are in control of your self-esteem.	5. Bullying can lead to low levels of self-esteem, depression, and even suicide.
6. Bullying stops once you leave school behind.	6. In a 2014 national survey conducted by the Workplace Bullying Institute, 27 percent of those surveyed had current or past experiences with abusive conduct at work. More startling is that 72 percent of Americans are aware of workplace bullying.[16]
7. Doesn't workplace bullying generally involve men bullying women?	7. Some men bully both men and women. However, according to a 2014 survey, 68 percent of the cases reported involve woman-on-woman bullying.[17]
8. Bullying is no worse than teasing.	8. Teasing is intended to be fun and often involves laughing *with* someone. Bullying is intended to be offensive, humiliating, and to make others feel bad and often involves laughing *at* someone.

APPENDIX C

Definitions of Bullying

Because bullying has not been deemed a violation of law (unlike sexual harassment), there is no uniform, generally accepted definition as to what constitutes bullying. Below are a few definitions from a variety of sources.

"Someone who intimidates and hurts others"[18] (Marianne Johnston).

"Anyone who abuses his power or position"[19] (Nick Vujicic).

"Bullying is a distinctive pattern of deliberately harming and humiliating others, specifically those who are in some way smaller, weaker, younger or in any way more vulnerable than the bully"[20] (*Psychology Today*).

"They overcontrol, micromanage, and display contempt for others, usually by repeated verbal abuse and sheer exploitation"[21] (Harry Levinson, PhD).

"Bullying is offensive, intimidating, malicious, or insulting behavior involving the misuse of power that makes a person feel vulnerable, upset, humiliated, undermined, or threatened.

'Power' does not always mean being in a position of authority, but can include both personal strength and the power to coerce through fear or intimidation. Bullying can take the form of physical, verbal, and nonverbal conduct"[22] (*NAVEX Global*).

"The malicious verbal mistreatment of a target that is driven by the bully's desire to control him or her"[23] (Gary Namie).

"A continual and relentless attack on other people's self-confidence and self-esteem"[24] (Tim Field).

"Bullying is the act of diminishing another's self-worth through physical, verbal, or nonverbal means for the purpose of intentionally insulting, humiliating, or harming that human being" (Mary Rauchenstein).

APPENDIX D

Resources

1. National Suicide Prevention Lifeline—1-800-273-TALK (8255).

2. Centers for Disease Control and Prevention (CDC) Suicide Prevention website—http://www.cdc.gov/violenceprevention/suicide/.

3. "Depression and Coping with Suicidal Thoughts," familydoctor.org, http://familydoctor.org/familydoctor/en/diseases-conditions/depression/symptoms/coping-with-suicidal-thoughts.printerview.all.html.

4. US Department of Education's Safe Schools—Healthy Students Initiative, http://www2.ed.gov/programs/dvpsafeschools/index.html.

5. Mental Health in Schools (A Quick Center Training Aid: Bullying Prevention), http://www.smhp.psych.ucla.edu/pdfdocs/quicktraining/bullyingprevention.pdf.

6. StopBullying.gov at http://www.stopbullying.gov/.
7. Pacer Center's Teens against Bullying—http://www.pacerteensagainstbullying.org/tab/.

APPENDIX E

Join the Revolution

The good news is that all states (according to www.stopbullying.gov) have enacted antibullying laws and/or policies that protect children from being bullied at school. Not all states include cyberbullying, which seems odd, given that in a 2014 study, 25 percent of teenagers reported they'd been bullied via the Internet or through texting. Over 52 percent of young people surveyed reported that they had been cyberbullied, 55 percent of teens who use social media reported witnessing cyberbullying, and 95 percent of them ignored it.[25] This is a beginning, but much more work remains to be done to help schools change the social norms in which bullying is viewed as some sort of normal rite of passage for kids. It is also important to note that currently, there is no federal antibullying legislation.

We also need to address workplace bullying. In 2001, David Yamada, a Suffolk University professor of law, authored the original Healthy Workplace Bill. Gary and Ruth Namie, Carrie Clark, and Moe Tyler lobbied lawmakers in California in 2002. The Healthy Workplace Bill has been modified since then and has been introduced in more than half of our states. While it has yet to become law in any state, there is momentum. Check to see the activity in your state by visiting http://healthyworkplacebill.org/.[26]

If you would like to lead and have a desire to see legislation passed that outlaws workplace bullying too, I applaud you. Some momentum has been generated. Reach out to your state legislators to keep the ball rolling! We each have a voice, and when it's heard, we *can* make a difference. But let's face it: while one voice can make a difference, the journey can take time. Time has a way of creating indifference. And indifference kills passion. If we combine our voices, we can create a beautiful sound that won't be silenced!

How about it? Are you ready to join the revolution to put an end to bullying?

I want to thank my friend Harold Thomas, an author and political consultant, for providing the following recommendation and links to congressional representatives. He advises against pursuing *federal* antibullying legislation as a starting point, as it is easier and more in alignment with the Constitution to press for *state* antibullying legislation. To find your legislators by state, visit http://openstates.org/find_your_legislator/.

To find your legislators by zip code, go to http://www.house.gov/representatives/find/. If your zip code falls in more than one congressional district, you will be asked for the "zip+4" code.

Acknowledgments

I'm grateful to my husband, Paul, who has always been my biggest supporter. He encourages me to dream big and not let others diminish my goals. I'm also grateful to Warren Planitzer, Bill Dolan, Mike Fitzpatrick, Ken Mills, and Cameron James. You all led from a place of respect and authenticity. I've learned a great deal from each of you and believe that I'm a better leader today because of the lessons you presented to me. I also wish to thank my collaborative publisher, Kary Oberbrunner. Thank you for giving me a voice and a platform to speak about an important topic. Thank you, Harold Thomas, for your guidance in legislative efforts. My heartfelt thanks and appreciation go to editors Diane Freeman and Alison Forche and to my proofreaders Lorraine Jusino, Reg Bush, Bill Bush, Jenny Rauchenstein and Paul Rauchenstein. You all helped make this a better book! In addition, I can't imagine growing up without my siblings Reg, Bill, Bob (whom we lost in 2016), Tom, Jim, and Diane. While we've been scattered across the country for many years, your love and support has been a timeless gift. To my extended family and friends, my love and appreciation to all of you for your support and encouragement in completing perhaps the most important item on my bucket list! And finally, I dedicate this book to the families of those children who have taken their lives as a direct result of having been bullied. Sadly, there are too many names listed (on the following page)—and many more that are not listed. May this book serve the purpose of keeping others off the list.

In Memoriam

Daniel
Bart
Katelyn
Slajana
Hope
Grace
Emily
Tyler
Brandy
David
Ryan
Nicola
Audrie

Rebecca
Megan
Jamey
Amanda
Ronan
Erin
Emilie
Alyssa
Dominique
Marie
Jamie
Phoebe
Kelly

Hannah
Eric
Kenneth
Dawn
Rachael
Jadin
Carlos
Sarah
Jessica
Laura
Matthew
Rehtaeh

Endnotes

[1] Sandra Graham, "Bullying: A Model for Teachers," American Psychological Association, accessed March 13, 2015, http://www.apa.org/education/k12/bullying.aspx.

[2] "WBI Survey: Workplace Bullying Health Impact," Workplace Bullying Institute, August 9, 2012, accessed May 29, 2015, http://www.workplacebullying.org/2012-d/.

[3] Pamela Hall, *Making a Bully-Free World* (Minneapolis, MN: Magic Wagon, 2014), 10.

[4] Ibid.

[5] "The Seven Catholic Sacraments," American Catholic, accessed July 14, 2015, http://www.americancatholic.org/features/special/default.aspx?id=29.

[6] "Risk Factors and Warning Signs," American Foundation for Suicide Prevention, accessed May 21, 2015, http://afsp.org/about-suicide/risk-factors-and-warning-signs/.

[7] Ibid.

8 W. E. Copeland, A. Angold, E. J. Costello, and H. Egger, "Prevalence, Comorbidity, and Correlates of DSM-5 Proposed Disruptive Mood Dysregulation Disorder," *The American Journal of Psychiatry* 170 (2013): 173, accessed May 6, 2015, http://ajp.psychiatryonline.org/doi/full/10.1176/appi.ajp.2012.12010132.

9 "The Relationship between Bullying and Suicide: What We Know and What It Means for Schools," CDC, National Center for Injury Prevention and Control, last modified April 2014, accessed August 3, 2015, http://www.cdc.gov/violenceprevention/pdf/bullying-suicide-translation-final-a.pdf.

10 Amy Maxmen, "Secret Shame—Do You Fear What Others Think of You? How Shame Can Hurt Your Health," *Psychology Today*, posted October 26, 2007, accessed January 23, 2016, https://www.psychologytoday.com/articles/200710/secret-shame.

11 "The Relationship between Bullying and Suicide."

12 "ZeroRisk HR Pre-Employment Test and Assessment Services," ZeroRisk HR, accessed December 15, 2015, http://www.zeroriskhr.com/.

13 "Who We Are," Toastmasters International, accessed January 27, 2016, http://www.toastmasters.org/About/Who-We-Are.

14 "The Relationship between Bullying and Suicide."

15 Stephanie Pappas, "Popular Kids Face Greater Risk of Getting Bullied (STUDY)," LiveScience, Huffington Post, April 1, 2014, accessed March 13, 2016, http://www.huffingtonpost.com/2014/04/01/popular-kids-more-at-risk-for-bullying_n_5070487.html.

16 Gary Namie, Daniel Christensen, and David Phillips, "2014 US WBI Workplace Bullying Survey," Workplace Bullying Institute, February 25, 2014, accessed January 5, 2016, http://www.workplacebullying.org/2014-wbi-us/.

17 Ibid.

18 Marianne Johnston, *Dealing with Bullying* (New York: The Rosen Publishing Group, 1996), 5.

19 Nick Vujicic, *Stand Strong* (Colorado Springs, CO: Waterbrook Press, 2014) 5.

Endnotes

[20] "Understanding Bullying," *Psychology Today*, accessed January 15, 2016, https://www.psychologytoday.com/basics/bullying.

[21] Hara Estroff Marano, "When the Boss Is a Bully," *Psychology Today*, posted September 1, 1995, accessed January 15, 2016, https://www.psychologytoday.com/articles/199509/when-the-boss-is-bully.

[22] "Global Anti-Harassment and Bullying Policy Sample," NAVEX GLOBAL, 2014, 3, accessed November 8, 2015, http://www.navexglobal.com/issues/harrassment-discrimination.

[23] Gary Namie and David C. Yamada, "Healthy Workplace Bill," The Healthy Workplace Campaign, accessed August 20, 2016, http://healthyworkplacebill.org/.

[24] Kasi McLaughlin, "Workplace Bullying—A Silent Epidemic," *Ezine Articles*, posted December 18, 2008, accessed July 4, 2017, http://ezinearticles.com/?Workplace-Bullying---A-Silent-Epidemic&id=1803999.

[25] "Cyber Bulling Statistics 2014, Finally!," NoBullying.com, December 2015, accessed January 15, 2016, http://nobullying.com/cyber-bullying-statistics-2014/.

[26] Namie and Yamada, "Healthy Workplace Bill."